WHO GETS PROMOTED WHO DOESN'T AND WHY

10 THINGS YOU'D BETTER DO IF YOU WANT TO GET AHEAD

DONALD ASHER

TEN SPEED PRESS
Berkeley

For Lisa

Ten Speed Press and the Ten Speed Press colophon are registered trademarks of Random House, Inc.

Some portions of this book originally appeared in other forms in the *Wall Street Journal's Managing Your Career* magazine and CareerJournal.com.
Reprinted by permission from Dow Jones & Co., Inc., and CareerJournal.com, the free executive career site from the *Wall Street Journal*.

Library of Congress Cataloging-in-Publication Data Asher, Donald.
    Who gets promoted, who doesn't, and why / Don Asher.
    p.   cm.
    Includes index.
    1. Career development—United States. 2. Promotions—United States. I. Title.
    HF5382.5.U5A75 2007
    650.1—dc22   2006037628

ISBN-13: 978-1-58008-820-6 (alk. paper)

Printed in the United States of America

Cover design by Ed Anderson/Scout Design
Interior design by Jeff Brandenburg/ImageComp

12 11 10 9 8 7 6

First Edition

TABLE OF CONTENTS

ACKNOWLEDGMENTS

I owe this book, really, to my clients, those fast-track careerists who so generously shared their experiences with me over the years. We plotted and schemed together. You went for it, and you beat out smarter, better, more attractive rivals to win advancement. You looked in the mirror and were honest about what you had to do to stay competitive. You were brave and courageous when it would have been so easy to choose to be corpulent, overpaid, and lazy. You rejected the status quo. You created your own next reality. It has been truly exciting to work with such ambitious, talented, smart, and genuinely charming individuals. Thank you.

This is my tenth book, and no one gets this far without backing. I am truly indebted to Ten Speed Press. They have stuck by me for all ten of these titles, an unusual run in the modern publishing world. Their loyalty may not have always been justified, but it has always been deeply appreciated. Fuzz, Phil, Lorena, George, and Jeff, you know who you are, and I want you to know I appreciate all you've done for me on this book and on all the others.

I want to acknowledge Bill Watkins, Sr., Tia Woodward, and Ellie Hall, some of the most brilliant businesspeople I know, for giving me fantastic interviews for this book. All of the careerists, executives, and H.R. officers I interviewed were more than helpful, and this book wouldn't have been any good without their wisdom and generosity.

And I am appreciative of Alan Ferrell, Director of Management Placement for Purdue University's Krannert Graduate School of Management. Alan, forgive me for misspelling your name in the last book, and check out your quote in this one! I hope I got it right.

Finally, I appreciate you, dear reader. I appreciate your willingness to try to control your own destiny, your desire to find rewards commensurate with your contributions, and your hankering for colleagues of the same fine caliber as you. Go for it! You deserve your success.

Who gets promoted in your company? The hard-working, quiet, reliable type who always delivers the extra mile? The glad-handing, politicking ne'er-do-well who has the boss's ear? The proven insider? Or the new blood from outside your department or function? The worthy person who waits her turn? Or the crafty fox who steals the chance?

There is a tremendous amount of mythology surrounding these questions. It seems that our beliefs about witchcraft and ghosts are more grounded in reality than much of what we "know" about promotions. This is partly the result of interpreting promotion events from our own point of view. We may see a promotion decision—either as an observer or an interested party—that doesn't make sense to us. So we rationalize: I didn't get the promotion because the boss favors men, we may say, or she favors women, people without kids, married people, people who are really good looking, and so on.

Certainly, every promotion event is different. Managers make decisions based on complex and unique data, using criteria that may apply only to the case at hand. But in aggregate, promotion decisions usually follow a pattern, and identifying that pattern can be of use to careerists trying hard to manage their own careers. My contention is that for every promotion event, there is a formula that determines the outcome of who gets the promotion. It may not hold in every single case, but it will hold in general.

I have long known that most people's ideas about who gets promoted and why were simply wrong. This book is the result of over twenty years of experience and accumulated wisdom helping highly motivated people manage their careers. I also conducted several hundred interviews with people who know the most about promotions: fast-track careerists who get promoted again and again; H.R. and line managers who face tough decisions every day about whom to promote and how to defend those decisions once they make them; but the most helpful interviews come not from those manning the gates of power, but from those who pass through those gates. H.R.

and line managers often operate on principles that they may not be able to articulate. You simply cannot send out a social science survey and generate the insights that come automatically with extended experience in the field. However, fast-track careerists can tell you *exactly* why they got chosen over their rivals. So a lot of what you will read here, the *secrets* to getting promoted, came straight from the strategists who have used these secrets to achieve their success.

But before I get to the secrets, let me give you a piece of essential advice that isn't a secret at all: Do your job, and do it well. That was the number one tip I got from surveying managers and careerists. While there will always be a few backstabbing connivers who ride their connections to advancement, in general, doing one's job well is the foundation to promotion. Because this should be obvious, it is not one of the chapters in this book.

This book is about the reality that doing your job is not enough to get promoted. In fact, just doing your job might be the biggest career mistake you could make. The question is, do you want to manage your career or just experience it? If your strategy is to follow your passion and hope that success will follow, you could toil away underutilized and unrewarded for years and years.

Because success is not just about working harder than those around you, by making small changes in strategy and small changes in the way you position and represent yourself, you can put the same amount of effort into your career and receive a vastly different return. Skills do not separate the very successful from the merely successful; strategy does.

There is probably a skillset difference between someone earning $35,000 per year and someone earning $85,000 per year. But *most* of the people earning $65,000 to $85,000 have the same job skills as someone earning $200,000 to $300,000 per year. So who makes it past the bottleneck of middle management? People who know the secrets to getting promoted.

May you find success in these pages.

CHAPTER ONE

TIMING
IS AS IMPORTANT AS
PERFORMANCE
OR TALENT

A Promotion Is Not a Reward

Most people believe that getting promoted is a reward for past performance. This is absolutely false.

Employers are not rewarding strong performers for their *past* contributions; they are investing in their *future* contributions. The sooner you grasp this fundamental truth, the closer you will be to getting promoted.

So, no matter what you have done in the past, the boss really doesn't care. What she cares about is what you can do for her (and the company) in your new position. Your past only serves as an indication of what you might do in the future, *one piece of evidence*, at best. It is only what you may do in the future that drives the promotion decision.

One of the worst political campaigns I ever saw was for a local politician who had signs all over town that said: "Vote for X. She's *earned* it!" as if getting elected were something you earn. You do not earn a promotion by *past* performance. You prove you are the optimum choice to deliver *future* performance.

This was basically Bob Dole's campaign for president in 1996. His campaign could be reduced to this slogan: "Vote for Bob Dole. It's his turn," the presidential equivalent of "He's earned it." The voters chose a future with clearer definition, and Bill Clinton went on to an eventful second term.

So you don't bank Brownie points to get promoted. If you've been working hard and are still waiting to be noticed and rewarded, you may be in for disappointment. Promotions are the ultimate case of "What have you done for me lately?" In fact, employers really don't want to know what you've done, even lately. They want proof that you can deliver a specific, clearly targeted future.

Right now, all over the world, there are angry, frustrated people who have been passed over for promotions—passed over in spite of their loyalty, performance, skills, and belief that they'd earned it and it was their turn.

To get promoted, you have to offer the best future out of the available options.

Why the Best Person May Not Get the Promotion

Companies don't hire the best person for the job; *they optimize the outcome of the staffing change.* So not only are you competing with all the other people who may want the new job, you're competing with the company's impression of the benefits of leaving you where you are versus the risks of giving you the promotion.

If you're more valuable where you are, you won't be getting that promotion.

Even if you have the entire skillset they need for the new position, there are several reasons you might be more valuable where you are:

- ☐ Promoting in-house creates two staffing changes; hiring from the outside involves only one.

- ☐ Your skills may be rare and difficult to replace, while the new job requires skills that are rather easy to procure from someone else. (This may be true even if the new job pays significantly more.)

- ☐ If you have created a feathered nest with your personal stamp on every aspect of what you do, staff that is loyal only to you, procedures known only to you, and so on, dislodging you could be too disruptive to the organization.

- ☐ You may be in the middle of a critical, high-value project, and your removal would be too disruptive.

- ☐ External customers may be addicted to you, and your reassignment could exact too high a cost from those relationships.

- ☐ You may be so efficient and cost-effective where you are that managers fear your removal may invoke large and unpredictable costs.

Cost has many factors. Some of the most significant costs associated with staffing changes are recruiting and onboarding a replacement as well as disruption to the existing functions managed by the employee who might be promoted.

Human resources professionals have gotten pretty good at estimating direct recruiting and onboarding costs for hiring different levels of staff: At the executive level, a common H.R. rule of thumb is that it will cost 1.5 times the annual salary to recruit and onboard a corporate officer or function head. Even a receptionist can cost thousands of dollars in recruiting and agency fees, testing, management time for interviewing, training, and so on.

If it costs more to replace you than to hire someone else, they'll hire someone else.

One way to tip this analysis in your favor is to keep the company from running two simultaneous placement efforts—*or any at all*. Offer yourself for the promotion *before* a search is launched for the desired position so you can cite those savings as part of your rationale. If possible, identify someone ready, willing, and qualified to replace you to further reduce the cost of promoting you.

The cost of the disruption of your leaving a current assignment is harder to estimate and often much greater than the cost of outside recruitment. The loss of productivity when a strong performer is taken from a unit can have a significant impact on that unit's bottom line, and even a talented incoming manager may face a long learning curve before hitting his stride in a new assignment. (If companies had accurate data on these costs, they'd spend a lot more time and energy on retention.)

Because the costs of staffing adjustments are not easily estimable, most managers just throw them into risk analysis. But cost and risk are not the same thing. Costs are estimable, finite, and numeric; they're not scary. Risks are, by definition, scary, unknown, and unpredictable. A manager who might not at all fear the cost of promoting you, might blanch at the *risk* of promoting you: What is the worst thing that can happen if we promote Karen? Will she succeed in the new unit? Will her old unit fall apart? Is she gunning for my job? Will she leave the company anyway?

The risks associated with promoting you must be manageable and perceived as less horrific than the risks associated with hiring or promoting someone else.

You must provide more benefits and fewer costs and risks than the other choices your manager has. Most people seeking a promotion pay more attention to promising benefits than they do to alleviating costs and mitigating risks, but all three are critical in any decision to promote from within.

DECISION VECTORS INFLUENCING PROMOTION DECISIONS	
Perceived <u>cost</u> of promoting you → ←	Perceived <u>cost</u> of promoting or hiring someone else
Perceived <u>risk</u> of promoting you → ←	Perceived <u>risk</u> of promoting or hiring someone else
Perceived <u>benefit</u> of promoting you → ←	Perceived <u>benefit</u> of promoting or hiring someone else

You must pass all three of these vector tests to be promoted. Sometimes an internal candidate passes two of the three criteria: Perhaps she can be replaced at modest cost and promises to be a strong contributor, but the risk is too great.

Top performers are often passed over because of the risk factor. Top performers are by definition not like the rest of us. Many are difficult and temperamental people. They've lived in a world designed for the averages; they are often frustrated, or they may be rule breakers. Are you known as reliable? Or are you a strong contributor with a tragic flaw, like a hot temper or a habit of blowing off assignments that don't interest you? When managers do risk analysis, they must project worst-case scenarios. If the risk is too great, all the benefits in the world will be passed over in favor of a less risky alternative.

Also, note the use of the term "perceived" in Figure 1.1. **Perception is reality** when it comes to management. If management perceives you as risky, highly talented, diligent, or prone to gaffs, then that perception is your reality. So you need to worry about how others *perceive you* at least as much as you worry about your work. We'll have more to say about this in later chapters.

Why Buddy Didn't Make Sales Manager

Buddy R. was the top salesman at a Ford dealership. He sold twice as many cars as any two other sales reps. Buddy had three talents that made him number one: First, he had a knack for establishing rapport with customers of any background. He could sell a new Crown Victoria to a neurosurgeon in the morning and a used F-150 pickup to a construction worker with limited English that afternoon. Second, he had the ability to remain focused on one sale at a time, giving him a high one-visit sales rate and reducing the need to share commissions with other reps who might end up taking over a handoff. Third, he had a genius for spotting buyers. He could look across the lot and tell you who was just a tire kicker and who would buy a car that day. Buddy only approached buyers.

So why was Buddy passed over for sales manager? Buddy came in late, he skipped "mandatory" sales meetings, he ignored his assigned floor duty, and walked right past customers he didn't think were going to buy, in effect dumping them on the other reps. Buddy was an unapologetic prima donna sales god who got away with behavior that would get other reps fired. They all resented Buddy. And one of them got promoted instead of Buddy.

Why Madison D. Didn't Make Partner

Madison D. was an attorney at a Manhattan-based boutique firm specializing in complex family trusts and estates. She was a star performer, seemingly with the whole package. She worked long hours. She was good at staff development and ran a tight team. She was one of the firm's top billers *and* a rainmaker. All of this should have put her in the running to make partner. So why was Madison passed over again and again?

Ironically, it was because of her rainmaking technique: Madison trolled for new clients in bars frequented by Wall Street types.

The partners loved all the new accounts, but they worried about her drinking. Since the firm specialized in services for high-net-worth families (trusts and estates), they were particularly sensitive about their reputation. So, again, a top performer was denied promotion because of a risk analysis.

Why Timing Matters So Much

Suppose you have no fatal flaws, you've anticipated and acquired the needed skillset, and you are a well-regarded standout among your peers. So how could you be passed over for promotion? Simple: You may be the best person for the job, but you may not be *available* to take the job! Whether a promotion involves filling a new position or replacing an existing one, the organization is going to want that job filled on a specific schedule. There may be some flexibility, but if you cannot be extracted from your current duties *to achieve a smooth handoff within the window of opportunity,* someone else will be getting the new assignment.

Ambitious people tend to get critical assignments. But if having a full plate keeps you from appearing available when a new opportunity arises, you'll be passed over, possibly in favor of some laggard who appears to have plenty of time to take on new duties.

People who get promoted again and again tell me that working the clock is a critical skill. You might get lucky once or twice in a career and have your availability magically coincide with an internal opportunity, but the most successful people *systematically* make themselves available as opportunities arise.

Three factors come into play here:

1. Anticipating the upcoming opportunity

2. Drawing your work to some kind of closure

3. Having a replacement ready to take over your old job

Anticipate Change and Offer Yourself as the Solution

You need to know about internal opportunities *before they're posted.* Once an opportunity is posted, several things have already happened: A lot of competition will have been alerted to the opportunity, and you will have to be demonstrably better than anyone else to get the assignment. Worse than that, H.R. will have gotten involved. A position description and skillset analysis will have been written that may not favor you, and there will be a process and a timeline assigned for making a placement that might not match your availability. So waiting for a posting has definite downsides.

People who manage their careers, as opposed to just experience them, process more information than other people. They see beyond their own tasks and job. They see an intertwined network of internal and external forces working on sectors of the organization. They *anticipate* senior management moves.

In short, they have a nose for change, and they place themselves in front of that change, ready to capitalize on it and contribute to the organization's response to that change.

Whether the change is positive or negative is not that important. It's the change itself that creates the opportunity for advantage. An aggressive careerist can turn even an apparent disaster to his advantage. For example, if the company is going to move an entire business unit offshore, most of the people in the unit would consider that a disaster. But a real careerist would see it coming and either jump to another unit before the RIFs begin or become the person managing the offshoring process and perhaps even continue as an HQ liaison to that overseas function.

How Mary C. Got Promoted to Assistant Dean

Mary worked in administration for an old-line college on the East Coast. She had had several assignments of increasing responsibility in both housing and student affairs but just couldn't break out of the "coordinator" and "administrator" title cluster. Through her many connections, she began to hear rumblings that the president thought the institution had too many layers of administration and too many career employees whose hearts weren't really in service delivery.

So *on her own* she researched organizational consultants who were active in higher education and called same-level colleagues at other institutions and asked them what had happened in reorganizations. While most employees ignored the president's signals, she got on his calendar, dropped the names of several consulting firms, described events at other institutions that had addressed administrative stagnation, and even volunteered to do a white paper if he was interested, making it sound like it would be no big thing. He was interested. When she presented her findings on best practices and academic restructuring, she made it clear that she was interested in managing such a project, and sure enough, when a pilot restructuring project came up, Mary C. got the assignment, along with the title of 'acting' assistant dean. When the project turned out to be a success, she got the "acting" dropped. In the end she restructured the entire student services function.

She accomplished her long-term goal by taking a series of small steps: She anticipated institutional needs, developed a knowledge base on her own and ahead of anyone else, volunteered to solve a problem before anyone else got the assignment, and thus had already *proven* her *future value* when the opportunity to pilot the project arose.

She got promoted in a bureaucratic, seniority-laden system, while older workers with better credentials were still "waiting their turn." Hers is a textbook example of how to get promoted.

Which Changes Will Affect You?

We'll talk more about how to get this information in the next chapter, but for now, let's consider changes that are typical in any organization and how they might affect you. Their power to impact you depends on where you are in the org chart. If you are a senior person, you need to worry more about potential staffing changes at the top, external forces, competitors, and the economy as a whole. If you are just starting in your career, you need to worry more about your department, your immediate work area, and the personalities of the people closest to you. And everybody needs to worry about the alignment of one's duties with organizational strategy and priorities. If you're working on something that becomes unimportant, you're at risk whether you are a strong performer or not. On the other hand, if you succeed with a project that is critical to advancing an organizational goal, that contribution *will* get noticed.

So the question is: Are you avoiding learning something that you need to know to make it to the next level? Has your boss dropped any hints about further training to acquire a new skill? If so, you'd better pay attention. The alternative to advancement is not always stagnation—sometimes it's removal.

The following are some examples of observations that, if acted upon, can give you the edge.

- ☐ Your competitor is about to launch a product or service similar to the one you've been working on.

- ☐ A critical worker is about to retire.

- ☐ Your company's revenues have tanked, and budgets are going to be a problem.

- ☐ You hear through the grapevine that a coworker interviewed with another company for a job.

- ☐ A new manager is coming on board one, two, or even three levels up from you.

- ☐ A critical worker one or two steps up from you is pregnant and may be taking maternity leave during a time a critical project is due.

- ☐ The company bought a competitor or vendor and needs to integrate or reorganize the acquisition.

- ☐ Your boss gripes about a problem, or your boss's boss gripes about a problem.

- ☐ The company wants to commercialize a product, enter a new market, start exporting, install CRM, become ISO certified, or the like.

Of course you should read the internal job postings on your company's intranet every day with your morning coffee, but it is *anticipating* organizational needs that drives a true competitive advantage. Once that posting is public—even internally—you're going to face competition, an existing job description, and managers who have envisioned a solution that may not look like you.

Once you hear about or conceive of a possible opportunity, to position yourself to execute a solution, you will need to establish three things with your boss:

1. You have or can get the needed skills and resources.

2. You are available.

3. Your assignment or reassignment will not disrupt your current area of work.

You Must Have (or Need to Get) the Necessary Skills and Resources

When it comes to skillset, have a little confidence in yourself! Don't over-estimate the requirements. Getting a friend to show you how some software works may enable you to grab an opportunity, while waiting to take a training program may allow the window of opportunity to slam shut.

Of course you should go to training classes and conventions, but the point is, don't delay pitching yourself for an opportunity, because timing is so critical. If you wait to develop deep expertise, you'll be useful to the person who was hired to solve the problem while you were gaining deep expertise.

And you have to have more than skills, anyway. You have to bring ideas to each endeavor. There are plenty of employees who make great soldiers implementing someone else's plans. But the people who advance quickly bring ideas and can create plans. So when you approach a boss about a problem, offer yourself as the solution to that problem.

Always provide more than one possible solution to a problem. Don't hesitate to walk into your boss's office and say, "I wonder if we could solve this problem by _____ or _____ or _____." Be flexible in the give and take of decision-making. *Don't love any one idea more than you love solving the problem!* Let your boss participate in the solution, developing your idea into one she can own. The smartest subordinates can walk into their boss's office and say, "I think we should paint the walls green, the color of money!" and before they leave, they'll have convinced their boss that the whole thing was the boss's idea in the first place. More commonly, the boss will take your idea, change it, and begin to formulate a plan to implement it. Do your best to be the instrument of that change.

You Have to Be Available!

Being available can be crucial. A friend of mine was up for advancement in the H.R. department of a large bank. She was a superstar who everyone thought was being groomed to be the future head of the department. But she missed a key promotion because she was put in charge of a headquarters move that made her unavailable for one full year. Right in the middle of that year, her dream assignment came up but was awarded to one of her rivals.

During that year, the bank went global, putting its first branches in Taiwan and Singapore, hiring its first offshore workers, and setting up its first offshore H.R. function. That was the assignment she missed. A headquarters move is critical, but not sexy. Going global is sexy, and she missed out.

You have to be able to draw your work into some kind of closure, and hand it off, to be promoted. If a rival is ready and you're not, she may get the nod while you are passed over.

The savvy careerist intentionally finishes projects just as a promotion becomes actionable. He'll speed up, slow down, hand off, • or whatever it takes to make the timing work. Managing time in concert with the needs of the larger organization can make a huge difference in career advancement.

You want to be the person senior managers think of automatically when new opportunities come up. You have to be seen as someone who can *finish* projects. Follow-through, completion, and being ready to pick up the next project—this is the description of *you* that you want in the minds of the decision makers.

Never Be Irreplaceable

In order to minimize any problems associated with leaving your old assignment, as well as maximize your attractiveness for the projected new assignment, never be irreplaceable.

Irreplaceable people are *never* promoted. You may be on a critical assignment that makes you temporarily irreplaceable, but in every organization there are some irreplaceable people who are intentionally so. To make themselves feel important and indispensable, they withhold critical data from others, refuse to delegate anything but the most mundane tasks, and retain all decision-making authority. They actually create a scenario in which their absence from work, for even a day, brings their unit or department to a halt until their return.

They are often talented people actually working at assignments below their abilities. By creating complexity in a function that doesn't necessarily require it, they appear indispensable. Or they may be limited in their organizational and procedural abilities, preferring to embody in themselves all the structure that their function may require. Over time, they've come to *be* their position rather than serve in it.

Irreplaceable people are the long-tenured accounts-payable clerk who refuses to train anyone in his function; the trust officer at a bank who just "knows" all the accounts and all their arcane rules; the foreign sales rep who refuses to introduce any junior people to his accounts; the project engineer who withholds key information from her teams and thus will always be a project engineer; the legal secretary whose boss cannot get along without her. None of these people can be promoted.

To be a fast-track person you need to make yourself easily replaceable. To accomplish this you will need to:

☐ Document your job.

☐ Train and develop your subordinates.

☐ Cross-train your lateral colleagues to cover your position.

☐ Pick a lieutenant and be sure she is ready to step into your shoes.

Documenting your job means that you have written procedures for everything you do, ready and available for your replacement. Policies, procedures, techniques, decision triggers, suppliers, vendors, the secret sauce recipe, all of these can be compiled in binders or intranet files. These, plus the assurance that you will be available to answer questions, can be a one-way ticket to advancement.

Be generous training and developing your staff. As your staff becomes better able to cover for one another, your organizational systems will be more successful. Relying on structures to get work done is safer than relying on personalities. And anybody who relies on heroes or irreplaceable people is at their mercy.

I once had a contract with AT&T to teach internal job-seeking skills to all the workers in a business unit. I thought the unit manager was crazy, that he would lose all his best people. He pulled me aside and said, "AT&T has just decided that a major identifier of executive talent is going to be how well we develop subordinates to take on leadership roles after they leave the unit. I'll take care of training and developing them, and you be sure they get promoted. I've got some really good people right now, and I think this can be a breakout move for my career." And it was.

In case you've never thought about it, teaching is a critical executive skill. CEOs spend a lot of their time making presentations, giving speeches, conveying ideas, and arguing against bad thinking in the organization. They are teachers in the truest sense of the word. Teaching, training, developing, guiding, and mentoring your subordinates can be career-advancing practices. And if you can't do this yourself, if you're not naturally a teacher, outsource the function to others within and outside your organization.

And you do not have to have a big staff or an important leadership role in order to implement this career strategy. You can start to become known as a trainer and developer of staff. If a new janitor is hired and you're already a janitor, volunteer to train the new hire. Training is a promotable skill, and it becomes more important, not less, as you rise up in the org chart.

You need to have your own succession plan. Who will replace you if you are promoted? If you have someone in mind, you can bring this information into the promotion equation. If you can be easily replaced because of timing factors or because you've done a good job of developing a subordinate or you have someone else in mind who could take over, you may get the nod even if your rival for the promotion is a much better performer.

Remember, organizations *optimize the outcome of the staffing change.* They don't hire or promote the best person for the job. Being easily and smoothly replaceable is, in fact, a major part of reducing the resistance to promoting you.

High performers are like engineers. They're always working themselves out of a job. There's an old joke among engineers: An engineer and a priest die together in a car accident. The priest is absolutely delighted with the afterlife. "This must be Heaven," says the priest. "Look at this magnificent city of gold."

"No, Father," says the engineer. "This surely must be Hell, for I can see that everything already works perfectly here."

INTERVIEW WITH AN ACCOUNT EXECUTIVE IN PUBLIC RELATIONS

Since I knew you were coming over today, I came up with my own Top Ten career points for the overly ambitious.

1. **The world is set up for early birds.** It's grossly unfair, but there is a halo around the employees whose biological clocks most resemble a rooster's. People respect the early birds because— let's face it—most of us aren't willing or comfortable getting up at 4 a.m. five days a week, and it makes those who are seem superhuman. Every minute that you arrive before the official start of the workday is worth at least fifteen of staying after the official end of the workday because nobody really cares if you work late. You can even leave at 5 o'clock as long as you beat the boss into the office in the morning. If you absolutely can't be early, then be consistently on time—but it's crucial that you show up before your support staff. How can you be seen as the leader if you are following your subordinates in the door each day?

2. **It is a fact that team players go far.** Managers like to promote team players (and conversely don't like to fire them) because

workplace morale stays high if a likeable person gets promoted but plummets if a jerk is advanced—even if the jerk is a great performer. Everyone in business wants to be treated well. Teamwork is recognizing that everyone is a valuable contributor and that you must treat the people you work with with the same respect that you would if you worked *for* them. It only takes one slighted secretary to stick a knife in your reputation. Remember, everyone is selling something, and people buy from likeable people. You don't have to be charming, but you should make an effort to cultivate relationships with those people you work with and for. Show that you genuinely care and give credit where it is due. Selfish people don't go far. Not everyone can be charismatic, but everyone can improve their likeability.

3. **Know when to keep your mouth shut.** In a typical work day, there are hundreds of opportunities to demonstrate your ignorance by talking too much. I once worked for a guy for over a year who barely ever spoke, but when he did, he slayed. He waited until he found an opportunity in a discussion for him to really contribute something. So instead of getting up to bat and striking out, he only hit home runs and was thought of as some kind of genius.

   The fact is that everyone interprets a simple sentence in their own way. After you say the valuable thing, shut up. Don't over elaborate or make the mistake of over explaining. Your effort to sound smart may just backfire.

4. **It's your client who writes your paycheck.** Your client's loyalty to you is your key to success. If the clients love you, your company will love you. And even if they don't, they won't be able to fire you without risking the relationship with the client. ***Make your clients love you and you make yourself bulletproof.***

   But don't mistake intimacy for a relationship. The superficial smiley face is not what I'm talking about. I'm talking about showing your clients, that you are their champion—that you have their back. Sucking up to your bosses is relatively worthless. Take care of your clients and they'll take care of your bosses.

And by the way, once you have a loyal client, ask for referrals. The only thing more bulletproof than a great client manager is a rainmaker.

5. **Sales matters in everything**. The bottom line, in business, is sales. Everyone sells: ideas, products, budgets, whatever—all the time. Don't wait for the proper time and place. You should be selling all the time, even if it's just "I thought I'd run this by you." And if you aren't completely sure who or how you will deliver, remember what a wise man once told me: Sell it first, then figure out how you're going to deliver.

6. **Don't waste energy trying to figure out how you're getting screwed**. I once worked with a very smart woman who had her MBA and years of practical experience, but she was **bitter**. When she wasn't working, she was looking for how she'd been screwed, how she might be getting screwed, or how she was going to get screwed in the future. We were at the same level in the organization, and when they gave us both new offices, she said, "It's about time." I wrote a short email to the president, cc'ing my boss and my boss's boss, thanking them all for my great new space. She is no longer with the company.

   There's no need to grovel, but it's important to have an *attitude of gratitude*. If they know that rewards and opportunities are well received, they are more likely to give you more.

7. **Understand rush season**. Every business has a crunch season—when your goods or services are in highest demand, when you will be staying late, working weekends, doing whatever it takes. Inevitably there are three basic employee reactions to this requirement: ignore it and leave at 5:00, grouse about it and trudge through, or roll up your sleeves and get it done. If you want to get ahead, you must understand that your extra effort during rush season isn't laudable. It's table stakes if you want to win. Even if you've delivered all year long, if you don't *really* deliver at crunch time, it's wasted. In the end, plodding doesn't get rewarded like sprinting. Periodic heroics are even better than daily reliability because they get you noticed.

8. **Demonstrate passion**. If I had a dollar for every job candidate I've interviewed that told me, "I'm passionate about this industry," I could afford the medicine I need to keep me from vomiting on the next one who says it. In reality, most workers are not passionate about their industry. There is a word for those who are: entrepreneurs.

   But there are employees who have a fire in their belly. They are exceptionally interested, exceptional people who think on their feet, create new solutions, and enjoy doing it. *They want to work.* If you are one of these people, you've got to let that show *internally* as well as with the client, because it doesn't count if nobody knows about it. Really successful people are as helpfully active within their organizations—in new business pitches, in morale- and team-building activities, in coaching and supporting—as they are with their external clients' businesses.

9. **Manage your review process**. Don't leave your work history to be written by your boss. Even if she likes you, she isn't the one carving the notches in your belt. It's up to you to record every accomplishment; keep your internal resume live, recording those bullet points as soon as they happen. If you don't keep a running record, you'll forget the small stuff, and it adds up.

   If you want a promotion, get on your boss's calendar six months prior to your review to discuss your career track and what it will take to get you to the next level. Don't make it a secret that you want to advance, or just assume it's going to happen. There may be good reasons why it can't happen this year, but you need to know what they are, so ask and then make any necessary changes or adjustments.

   The biggest mistake employees make is to think that promotions are given based on past performance. It's not what you've already done—it's what you can do next. The onus is on you to clearly show the benefit to them of promoting you. The fact of the matter is, the world is full of good administrative assistants, but it's hard to find a good business leader.

10. **Find your guardian angel**. The best career advice my father ever gave me was that in every organization, you need to have a guardian angel. They need to be several steps up from you, so

they can protect you if necessary. They must be someone who obviously likes you. The softer the spot they have for you, the better. Cultivate that relationship, but don't tax their time. Don't refer to them as your mentor—being a mentor, while flattering, is a responsibility and a general time suck that they may not be comfortable with. Show them that you are eager to learn from them if and when they have time to teach. It's up to you—not them—to manage the special relationship. Perhaps there is something you could do to lighten their load, but don't suck up. It's important that they understand that you're a person of integrity, and yours is a relationship of mutual respect, so some time when you really need them, your guardian angel can step in on your behalf.

That's everything I know about getting promoted, but I'm learning more every day. Come back and interview me again in a year.

CHAPTER TWO

YOU
HAVE TO
GET NOTICED

You *have* to be doing a great job in the assignment you already have. That's non-negotiable. If you aren't doing a great job where you are, don't even think about getting promoted. It's a nonstarter. So that's rule number one.

—H.R. Manager

WIN THE PROMOTION
PACKAGE YOURSELF FOR PROMOTION
BE AVAILABLE WHEN OPPORTUNITY KNOCKS
DEVELOP THE SKILLSET NEEDED FOR ADVANCEMENT
MAKE YOURSELF KNOWN TO THE RIGHT PEOPLE
DO YOUR JOB WELL

DOING YOUR JOB WELL IS THE FOUNDATION FOR ALL
FUTURE SUCCESS, BUT IT IS NOT ENOUGH BY ITSELF.

It's Not How Wonderful You Are. It's Who Knows You Are Wonderful

Do what you love, and the success will follow. That sounds like good advice, but it's not. If you're motivated and ambitious, and you want to get promoted, how do you get noticed? For your own boss to notice you, you'll need to do a better job than is expected, consistently, as a building block for your reputation. You don't have to be perfect, or even be good at everything you attempt, but when you are compared to your peers, you need to come up better by most measures most of the time. That's standing out, as in being outstanding. But is it enough just to do a great job? Absolutely not. That's one of the great career myths of our time.

If you don't sell your accomplishments and abilities, success may *not* follow. The world is full of outstanding performers stuck in go-nowhere jobs, working for semiconscious bosses who don't appreciate what they've got and have no plans to reward star performers. Why? Sometimes because they don't even know they have a star performer working for them.

You have to make sure that people know the good work you're doing, or your good work will have no career value. You may take great satisfaction in your good work, but you won't get promoted if no one knows what you can do.

How Ian R. Got Promoted to Art Director

Ian R. was an assistant art director for an advertising agency in the Northwest. The firm had one main account, a trendy athletic shoe company, for which it did everything from broadcast and print ads to managing sponsorship of sporting events. Ian's job was to line up some models to wear some new shoes for a test shoot and to order in some catering, but when he heard some top managers from the shoe company would be attending, Ian saw an opportunity.

Immediately he saw several problems with the shoot the way it was planned: (1) The models were going to be photographed full-length, which would minimize the shoes; (2) the eyeballs of the observers were going to be too far away from the shoes; (3) the shoes were waterproof, and although there had been some talk of having a model dash through a puddle, that shot had been scheduled for another location several days later. Ian was justifiably worried that the client would be unimpressed by the presentation.

First, Ian hired several members of the men's and women's swim teams from a local university and then he ordered the correct shoe sizes for each of them. Then Ian had an elevated platform built in the studio at sitting-eye level, with a shower connected to some plastic pipes, jury-rigged to drain into a bucket below the platform.

When the execs were brought in, they were seated in front of the platform hidden behind a red theatre curtain. Amid flashing lights and loud music, the curtain dropped, the swimmers danced a choreographed routine in the "shower," appearing to be nude behind a screen translucent from the knees up. Then the cameraman zoomed in on the only color in the frame: the dancing shoes, advancing right between two executives for a close up.

"Wow!" said the execs. "This is terrific! Who thought this up?"

And Ian was promoted to A.E. on the account.

I asked Ian how he learned to build portable showers inside a studio, and he said, "I was in a fraternity. We built stuff like this all the time for parties."

You Need a Communications Network

So how do you develop a communications plan to spread the word laterally and vertically? You need communication links outside of your boss and your direct reports because they are like your nuclear family; you *have* to talk to them—and you get no special credit for doing so. But your boss's boss should see your name regularly, and people in other departments and other functions should know about your successes, whenever you can make them known *gracefully*.

First content, then delivery.

To communicate to others effectively about yourself, you must manage your work history, and, so you don't forget any important details, it is important to keep up with your work documentation in real time. If you or your team or your department achieves a win, you need to go to your computer and—without being observed—log it onto your "brag sheet," which should be a private memo to yourself. You might even password protect it, to keep it from prying eyes. Log the accomplishment, and describe your role in it.

The smartest careerists tie their contributions to an overarching organizational goal or strategy. Don't just write down: "Debugged and released the RFID hand-helds." That's an IT goal. An organizational goal is tied to strategy, or the bottom line. So your brag sheet item should look more like this:

"Personally developed, tested, and released software used in three new in-the-field handheld computing devices allowing real-time data capture of product movement through RFID technology, reducing shipping errors, eliminating the last paper-based stages to our logistics chain, and achieving a 5 percent reduction in inventory carry costs system-wide. Since we were carrying $100,000,000 in inventory, 5 percent represents a $5,000,000 one-time savings and the equivalent of the borrow costs on $5,000,000 from this point forward. This was a critical milestone in advancing the company's goals to eliminate data entry from all processes, and to create seamless, real-time supply-chain logistics."

Your brag sheet will provide the building blocks for three types of documents that have critical external audiences: your annual review, your internal resume, and your external resume.

These documents should be updated and ready for release at all times. If you hear about a great opportunity that may be developing in a related department, you can drop your internal resume on that decision-maker and prevent him from posting the position on the intranet, or you may become the frontrunner and keep him from seriously considering others.

Some warnings: Rules govern internal job-seeking at most organizations. Some of these rules may be official, codified policies, while others are just prudent practice. If your current boss needs to be informed that you are speaking to someone about an opportunity elsewhere in the company, remember to show her that your departure will not be disruptive to your current unit, and talk about a future without you in your current role. It is a good idea to interview (internally) once in a while for something you haven't a prayer of winning, just to keep your boss used to the idea that you will be moving on.

Never let anyone see your external resume, and never admit that you have one ready. No gossip travels faster than a story about someone applying for a new job. Even an affair between two employees is easier to keep quiet. Be careful not to leave a printout in a copier, a printer, or on your desk. If you do hear about an external opportunity while in a group, follow up later when you are alone. Deny that you have an external resume ready, if the topic comes up. You can always say something like, "I probably have an old resume somewhere, but I'd need to update it."

Why Michael M. Didn't Get Promoted

Michael M. was up for promotion to executive vice president of worldwide operations for a software company. He had nailed the board interview, and the job seemed a lock. His final hurdle was a 360° review and an evaluation by an external psych consultant. The psych consultant gave a mostly positive assessment and recommended Michael M. for the job. But the review exploded like a cluster bomb. Michael's internal resume was shared with all the reviewers, and several of his coworkers objected to his taking credit for team efforts and the accomplishments of others! Michael was de-listed and was told by his own boss that "Some people up the ladder just thought you need a little more maturation before taking on a role as significant as this."

So treat your internal resume as a public document, and assume that it will be shared with all parties to a decision. Remember the grade-school rule: Don't write anything on an internal resume that you don't want to share with the whole class.

Working Hard When It Counts Most

If you are a recent college graduate, your greatest contribution will be your ability to work hard. Whatever your major, as a new hire your skillset will be pretty basic. Until you gain some experience, you won't be able to make massive contributions in terms of strategies or even tactics. But if you work hard, you will get noticed.

Remember that delivering the goods in crunch times buys you immunity. Dave Stewart was a starting pitcher for the Oakland A's during the ball club's heyday in the late 1980s. He had some truly mediocre seasons, but he was immune to being released for one reason: If the ball club made the playoffs, Dave Stewart could be counted on to win because he performed best under pressure. To watch him pitch in the playoffs was to see everything beautiful about baseball. His determination showed in his face. He glowered at batters with a withering scowl. He looked like the meanest man alive. He didn't throw pitches; he threw his contempt at the batters. And he got them out when it mattered. For the other 162 games, he might struggle, but in the playoffs, he was unbeatable.

Managing Expectations and Managing Perceptions

Managing expectations is a big part of career management, and it determines how you are perceived in a company. Is it better to underpromise and overdeliver or to make a big splash and hope you can produce what you've promised? It depends. If you're trying to make a deal—get an assignment, a new job, or a promotion—you *do* need to promise some benefits! On the other hand, if you already have a sure deal, it may be best to manage expectations and be a little more reserved. Either way, it is crucial to deliver on your promises once you make them. If you overpromise and underdeliver, you're not going to look like much of a hot dog.

And remember that talk *isn't* cheap—it can really cost you or reward you. Selling wins is a talent. I've gone to trade shows where I could have reported that we were in an obscure corner of the vendor maze, our neighbors were dullards, and the convention hosts busted us for selling products without an in-state sales license. Or I could have reported that we were the hottest booth in our area of the floor, driving twice or three times the volume of our neighbors, and we sold all our product even though some of the buyers wanted us to ship it to them later.

Both of these reports are accurate descriptions *of the same show.* The way you talk about your activities determines how you will be perceived!

It used to be that it wasn't a bad thing to be in the worst business unit in an organization. The theory was that it would be easier to make a noticeable difference. The problem is that companies today rather ruthlessly cut off failing business units, so asking for a tough assignment may be step one in getting you fired, even if you are, relatively, successful. More important, by going to the worst business unit you are robbing yourself of a chance to work closely with the best people. Talent sharpens talent. There's nothing more insufferable than a truly talented person who has been living in isolation, without the challenge and the balance of other talented people around her.

The Sure-Thing Promotion? No Such Thing!

Have you ever been up for a sure-thing promotion, when you were told it's yours but they just have to go through the motions? Bosses almost never make you "go through the motions" for no reason. Either they have some reservations or there is another decision-maker who wants to review the staffing change. Whatever they want you to do—submit a resume or go through an interview—take the process very seriously. A boss two levels up who has never met you may review your resume to see if you're seasoned enough for the assignment. There may be a ringer brought in to interview against you, and if you don't have the right answers and the ringer does, the tide may suddenly turn against you. It's never merely a formality! I cannot count the number of times someone I've known was up for a sure-thing promotion, only to have it unravel. You must show respect for the process, prepare properly for the interview, take care with your internal resume, and follow through crisply on everything that is asked of you. At this point, it's your job to make your boss look good. By making him look good, you make yourself look good to your new boss.

Four Rules for Hiring and Promotions

The Waiter Rule: Are you rude to service staff? Do you think this shows your superiority? Advice columnist Abigail Van Buren calls this a test of character. How you treat the people who have no power over you reveals your true character. Steve Odland, CEO of Office Depot, uses this test with all executive hires. If you're rude to the waiter, you don't get the offer. You don't have to be buddy-buddy best friends with support staff, but show character and be polite.

The Salt Rule: Do you salt your food before you taste it? Jack Welch, former CEO of GE thinks this is a sign that an executive would rush to judgment. If a candidate salted his food before taking a bite, he didn't get the assignment. You should assume that every aspect of your behavior is being observed when you're up for a promotion, and little details matter. And remember your dining etiquette: If someone asks for salt or pepper, pass them both.

The Airport Rule: Many hiring managers use the airport rule to make hiring decisions. If I were stuck in an airport on an eight-hour delay, would I want to be with this person? If the answer is "no way," you're in trouble. It pays to be able to have a discussion about more than one thing. Know a little about culture, a little about history, a little about current events, and you're likely to pass this test. In the modern, diversified workplace, sports blather and bad jokes won't get you very far.

The Beer Rule: This is very much like the airport rule, but you don't have to stay alive as long. Of the final two or three candidates, which one would I most like to have a beer with? If the answer is you, you're definitely still on the short list. People who are pleasant, comfortable in their own skin, and in possession of a working sense of humor really do have an advantage. Check your recent history: This is how Americans picked their president.

You Have to Get Noticed to Get Promoted!

So now you have your brag sheet up to date, how do you stand out? While interviewing highly successful people for this book, I was struck by how many of them brazenly walked up to top officers in the company and introduced themselves.

> An engineer heard the president of the company was visiting his manufacturing plant, and he barged into the plant manager's office and introduced himself. This later kept him from being laid off.
>
> One woman was on a golf outing and walked up to the top officers in the company, "I see you don't have a woman in your foursome. How about you pick me and that'll make it fair." Since there were *no* other women on the outing, this was a ludicrous rationale! But it worked. She stayed and played.
>
> A young man was part of a board presentation on EU marketing efforts. His job was to wear the right suit and place charts on an easel. After the presentation he walked up to the president and the CEO and told them how much he enjoyed working for the company. He also told them he was trilingual, and if any opportunities came up in the future where they needed someone who spoke French or German, he was ready to help.

Never pass up a chance to introduce yourself to senior officers whenever you have the opportunity.

You, Your Job, and Your Career

One of the main contentions of this book is that managing your career is not the same thing as doing your job. You can be great at doing your job but be simultaneously neglecting or even destroying your career. *They are separate processes.* On the other hand, if you spend *more* time managing your career than doing your job, you may endanger both. So there has to be a balance.

Most people do not worry about managing their careers. They mostly follow the Woody Allen rule—"Eighty percent of success is showing up"—so they just show up, put in their time, and take home a paycheck. By the way, this is no less true at the top echelons at many organizations.

So what about that other 20 percent of success? A big part of it is being intentional about your career and viewing it as a separate entity from you and your job that needs care, attention, and managing.

Let's separate the three entities of you, your job, and your career, and take a closer look at them.

You ≠ job. You are not your job. No matter how ambitious you are, let go of that idea right away. You are a complex person with aspects of your personality that could never find adequate expression at work. You have intellectual, social, sexual, spiritual, and artistic needs that it would be downright unwise to pursue at work.

You ≠ career. Likewise, you are not your career. If your career were to become interrupted due to illness (you can't work) or unbounded good fortune (you win the lottery or receive an obscenely huge inheritance), you would still be the same person. Your experiences might change, but your core personality would be going there with you.

Job ≠ career. Your job is certainly not your career. Your career will span many jobs, even if a lot of them end up being with the same organization. Your career is your strategy that ties together your jobs, and drives your decisions as you choose which opportunities to develop and pursue, and which to take a pass on.

For an ambitious careerist, there are complex interlocking webs of support and meaning between these three entities, but in the end they are totally separate one from another.

YOU, YOUR CAREER, AND YOUR JOB

YOU

YOUR CAREER

YOUR JOB

The Conversation

Once you've been on any job long enough to understand how to do it, and especially once you start to get some wins on your brag sheet, it's time to sit down with your boss for "The Conversation."

Before you set this up, be sure you know your boss's style. Is she someone who doesn't mind having impromptu meetings, even about serious matters, or is she someone who is going to want you to make an appointment? Pick an appropriate time and place to talk about your career, where you see it going, where you'd like to see it going, and most important, *ask for advice*. If you're smart, you'll listen more than you talk. Pay particular attention to these issues:

- ☐ **Career paths.** In almost all organizations, there are logical paths up the ladder. Position A leads to position B. Position 1 leads to position 2. But position 1 will not lead to position B, and position A will not lead to position 2, and so on. Learn where your career path is headed, and be sure that's where you want to go.

- ☐ **Skillset requirements.** No matter how brilliant and talented you are today, you will need to acquire knowledge and skills to excel in future assignments. Don't fight this; embrace it. Remember, you probably don't need to become an expert to advance; usually some exposure and basic skills will get you to the next level.

- ☐ **Personalities.** Who can help you? Whom should you avoid? What are the strengths and weaknesses of the gatekeepers to your future? Just be careful not to ask too many questions in this direction, or you'll look like you care more about politics than performance.

- ☐ **How you can do your job better.** Because success in your current assignment is a prerequisite for advancement, you should take every opportunity to discover how to do your job better, smarter, and easier.

Be prepared for your boss to take the opportunity of this meeting to let you know about her concerns and your shortcomings, and she may be annoyed that you think you can advance when she's been stuck there for years. But even if "The Conversation" doesn't go well, you need *that* information to manage your career. You'll know where you stand *now* in order to be able to make a strategy to get where you want to be in the future.

Here is what two MBAs told me about "The Conversation" they had with their bosses:

> "I was nobody special in my department until I sat down for that conversation. My boss took an interest in me after that and began to tell me how the department really worked. We started going to lunch together about once a month. I can trace everything that happened after that to that one meeting. Just the fact that I thought about my career, and where I was going, set me apart from a lot of the other new hires."

> "My boss told me that I was *not* going to get promoted out of my current assignment. He said that analysts are supposed to work for two years and then move on, and that's just how it is. The only people who even get third year promotions are graduates from the same Ivy League school as our founder, and I'm not. It hurt to hear that, but it did allow me to make a new strategy for advancing my career."

Sitting down with your boss to discuss your career will get you on her radar screen. You can also have conversations like this with other managers, and even people in other departments or divisions, but be careful that your boss doesn't think you're disloyal or trying to do an end-run around her to get ahead. (For more on this, see Chapter Six, "Always Make Your Boss Look Good.")

If you work for a small company or in a smaller business unit within a large organization, your career advancement may only be possible if you leave the company, department, or unit. It can actually work in your favor to discuss this with your boss, especially if she likes you and has begun to rely on your services, and especially if she has no plans of ever leaving her current assignment. It is important to be clear with her that you are moving on sooner or later and that you are not going to retire in position. A boss who "owns" you is not going to help you on your way; a boss who is just renting your services will. A rule of management is that anybody can be replaced, and a rule of career management is that all bosses will, eventually, be replaced. Be nice, be honest but not arrogant about your ambitions, and ask for help and advice. Usually you'll get it.

How Bobbie Lost His Boss's Respect

Bobbie R. went to lunch with his boss to discuss his performance and his career. He had been angling for months to set up the meeting, and to be sure he could get his boss alone with him. He even went to the trouble to discover his boss's favorite Italian restaurant. Then he proceeded to ruin the relationship, forever, by explaining how he was going to be earning $250,000 a year within five years, and he'd be in charge of at least multiple business units. Bobbie's boss had three kids in college and was still bumping along in middle management, struggling to cover his mortgage and all those tuition bills. Can you imagine what he thought about Bobbie?

The Problem with Young People

One of the common complaints about young people in the workplace today is that they need so much attention. They want constant reinforcement that they're doing okay. One manager complained to me recently, "It's the constant 'How'm I doing?' 'How'm I doing?' 'How'm I doing?' that drives me nuts. I'm lucky if I see my boss twice a month, but I have to review everything they do, sometimes several times a day."

More Ways to Get Noticed Higher up the Food Chain

Anything that makes you known—in a positive way—beyond your immediate boss and closest colleagues is good for your career:

Write well. Writing is a valued skill, so if you write well or even can just write clearly, that skill will stand out. Volunteer to craft materials for wide release, such as letters to clients or external stakeholders, policies, procedures, or manuals, product information, and so on. If you get the reputation of being a good business writer, managers and executives will seek your assistance with their projects. Writing carries your good performance to people who might never learn of you otherwise.

Speak well. Many a young person would do well to banish "like" and "you know" from their speech patterns, if they want to be taken more seriously. The proper answer to "thank you" is "you're welcome," not "no problem." If you mimic the speech of the people with power, you will be closer to having that power yourself.

The husband of a friend of mine complained bitterly about not being taken seriously at work, and I suggested he learn to speak faster. He looked at me like I had slapped him, but I explained: He had one of the most laconic speech patterns I had ever encountered. Although he was brilliant, his pace of speaking was a major impediment to the transmission of his ideas. I asked him if he could speak faster, and he admitted that he could; he had just never thought about it. I ran into him months later, and he said he could tell a marked difference in the reception he got at work when he spoke faster.

Your accent, or how fast you talk, can work for or against you. Accent reduction training is all that stands between many foreign nationals and true success. Area knowledge or technical expertise can get you hired, but to continue to advance you may have to take a class to reduce your accent so less-than-nimble American ears can understand what you are saying. The executive suite requires very different communication skills than a tech team. And although Arnold Schwarzenegger made it in the United States with his heavy accent, the very fact that everyone still talks about it is revealing.

Present well. Presentation teams often involve junior people who stand around not doing much. Try to get a speaking role in the next presentation you are supporting. Board presentations, client presentations, training and product demonstrations, and trade shows are all opportunities to stand out to company officers. They are a great way to meet people outside your department and provide opportunities for extended social interaction to boot. If you're not a confident speaker, get some training.

Travel. Business trips create exposure to senior people, to people outside your reporting channels, clients, and even other companies that might be a better match for you. You can build your network, find mentors and advisors, and "shop" for other employment opportunities.

Volunteer for everything. Well, almost everything. We'll cover this in greater detail in a later chapter, because often the best way to get noticed and promoted is to do your regular job *plus* cover a special project or some other simultaneous assignment. But be selective! Don't volunteer for assignments that will not be appreciated.

As a newbie, you pretty much have to do whatever you are assigned. But as soon as you have some latitude, be careful to avoid thankless tasks. A mechanical engineer that I interviewed for this book told me he started out as a quality-control engineer until he realized it was the worst kind of assignment. "If things are going well," he told me, "someone else will get the credit. When things start to go bad, you are responsible for sounding the alarm and for correcting the problems. So you are always associated with the foul-ups, and rarely with a feel-good success story." When he switched to project engineering, where almost every project resulted in a success story, his career took off.

Nail a special project. A strong performance on a special or unusual project has a much greater chance of being noticed than your regular day-to-day duties. Volunteer for such projects if they don't naturally come to you. But consider each opportunity carefully because some projects sound better and higher profile than they really are.

A director of a career center for a college told me the worst project he ever had was serving on the technology committee. They set multiyear standards for IT, including standardizing IT platforms campus-wide, and vetting and choosing all types of IT vendors. "It almost derailed my career," he told me. "Everyone hates new software, and so everyone hated everything we did. I mean, no one was happy with us." That is quintessentially the type of project to avoid.

So staying up all night photocopying presentation booklets might help you stand out as a newbie, but a long-term career strategy should be to focus your energy on high-value contributions. Besides, you'll be happier if you spend less time on unpleasant, unappreciated work.

Put in the hours. Coming in early, staying late, and showing face are critical career moves. Avoid telecommuting until you have carved your niche in an organization. And don't outsource or reassign quality if it directly affects your reputation. "Out of sight, out of mind" is a saying for a reason.

Deliver the goods. Stand-out performance will always help you get the stand-out assignments. Every boss values the worker who makes them look good.

Watch your credentials! If you are not constantly improving your skills, *your competition is.* Further training, certificates, continuing education, professional organization and trade show participation, can only work in your favor by adding to your skills and visibility and making you look serious about your career.

How Nicolas S. Got Noticed

After joining the marketing department of a large financial services company, Nicolas S. realized he was one of many hardworking bright young people in the department. He had a lot of competition to get noticed. But Nicolas had an edge. He had long been a superuser of PowerPoint, so he started offering his services to any manager in the company making a presentation. He attended a special training class called "The Visual Presentation of Quantitative Data." Nicolas became the go-to guy for all internal and external presentations. He did exactly what his company tries to do with all their products: he differentiated himself.

An Honest but Immoral Headhunter

I once interviewed a headhunter for a newspaper article who told me he doesn't advance people who are unattractive or unfit, and he actually used the "f" word, as in "fat." I was astounded that he would be so forthcoming. Fifteen minutes later he called back begging me not to use a word of the interview. As a gift to him, I agreed. (I am a business writer, not an investigative reporter.) But I never forgot. He's still a headhunter, well known and prosperous, and located in. . . .

Watch out for the Christmas party, or any party. A party can be a danger zone. A business party is *never* a social event; *it is a business event*, giving you a chance to meet and speak with company officers and prove your professionalism by drinking very little and heading home early.

Praise others—spread the credit. Praising others is a Trojan Horse for news involving you. Get in the habit of sharing the credit for your team's accomplishments, and you have a reason to send emails to officers further up the food chain.

But something I heard *repeatedly* from managers and company officers is not to abuse the cc function on email. Anyone you send email to should be in the normal channel for the information enclosed. Copying company officers to gain their attention with no other useful purpose can backfire. Which is why praising others is such a good habit to get into; it flows upward and is almost never seen as intrusive or suspicious.

Use service committees as another channel to shine. Don't avoid philanthropy assignments like the United Way drive as unpaid busywork. Besides being personally satisfying in community service, it can be another way to meet important people and to network.

Dress professionally. Although clothes don't really make the man, they say a lot about him. Dress as though you already had the promotion because dress conveys so much information about a person. It conveys power, a sense of prosperity, self-confidence, status, and social position in society. It conveys—in all its complexity—a person's self image. There is a reason we have the saying, "Clothes make the man." We have so codified our language that another name for a managerial-level man is "a suit."

Sociologists argue that clothes are even more important to and for women, who are even more attuned to the subtle signals in dress and adornment than are men. Certainly it is well established that women dress for other women and not for men, and if you stand outside the door of any major business, most women with more than passing fashion sense can tell you the relative rank and income of everyone coming through the door: "There's a secretary, there's a top executive, there's a computer techie of some kind, there's a clerk," and so on.

A concern when choosing someone for promotion is will he make a successful transition? Will he be able to do the job is only part of the equation. Will he be able to *become* the job is an even bigger question. Will he act right, represent himself and the unit well, and be a great reflection on the unit manager? By dressing as if you already have the promotion, you are removing one huge worry in advance. You already look right for the position. But keep in mind that you should not dress so much better than your boss that people assume *you* are the boss. This creates confusion among visitors and is overshooting the goal.

I do a lot of corporate training, and I have noticed that some people view training as an opportunity to ditch their business attire. This is unwise. If you want to be taken seriously, continue to dress better than those around you, whether you are in New York at HQ or at a meeting in Miami, in a conference room within sight of the pool.

Be ready at all times, which means having the right suit, the right reputation, the updated internal resume, and a rationale for why you are ready to advance, or take on more responsibility.

Develop a leadership demeanor. Leadership demeanor is an essential criterion for advancement in the military. Business, government, and nonprofits are no different. If you don't act like someone who has the promotion, it could result in your never getting a chance even to compete for it. Fortunately, *demeanor can be learned.* If the senior people in your company don't laugh loudly, you'd better not. If they are rather formal, you should be too. If the most successful people you observe stand and sit up straight at all times, so should you.

Demeanor can be situational, as in when you act one way with some groups of people and another way with other groups of people. You don't have to give up the "real" you; you just have to learn how to act like the person who is going to get the promotion—if the promotion is important to you. Even handshakes vary in intensity according to regions of the country and levels of status! Don't resent these truths; simply pay attention and adapt.

A renowned communications consultant I know reports that 55 percent of communication is body language, 38 percent is voice and tone, and only 7 percent is conveyed by the words you are using. Your body language, voice, and tone are critical parts of your leadership demeanor. Having the demeanor of those who have power will put you closer to having that power yourself.

Hygiene matters. I once knew a wonderful foreign bureaucrat who was moving to the U.S. with his American spouse. He spoke perfect English with a romantic accent that was easily understandable. He was handsome, well dressed, and he should have been able to find a good position, but I just could not get him to understand that Americans bathe every day. His response: more cologne.

Regular hair cuts, appropriate (which means light) makeup, appropriate (which means light) jewelry, the raincoat, the pen—all the details matter. I once knew a sales executive who tried to get job candidates to sign something, just so he could see what pen they had in their pocket. A cheap ballpoint stolen from the hotel was noticed. So was something nicer.

Avoid thankless tasks. A young accountant told me that in his office, filing was the worst kind of assignment. "We're switching to paperless, and so filing is like photocopying *War and Peace* one page at a time. And if you don't pay attention, and you smear a page or scan a Post It over a key number, you'll have to source the original and have it returned from storage. It's all downside, no upside. I never do filing. I'd rather shine the boss's shoes with my tongue."

One caution: Don't outsource or reassign quality if it directly affects your reputation. A young professional I interviewed for this book told me that her secretary tried to intentionally sabotage her career! She got promoted to her very first professional position and got assigned a lifer for a secretary. There were hints that this older frumpy white woman didn't really like working for a very young, very sharp black woman. This woman's secretary "lost" messages, misspelled powerful people's names in memos, cancelled meetings without telling her, and generally made her life a hell. "Once I figured out what was going on, I ran all my business through my cell phone. At first I couldn't believe it. 'Could this actually be happening?' I asked myself, and yes, it did happen. So until I could get rid of her, I just had to step in and do her job and my job, too." Verbum sat sapienti est.

I once tried to coach an acquaintance who cannot be promoted because he refuses to move from "nerd frump" to "manager neutral" in his dress. He dresses like a poor graduate student. So he cannot become a manager. He is stuck at the top of the techie compensation scale, which is comfortable enough, but cannot become an equity player because of this one problem.

Watch Out for Your Blind Spots

Few of us are born or educated into our fashion sense. We absorb it, like a sponge. And a sponge in dirty water absorbs a lot of impurities. All of this is a tortured way of introducing a problem that I have observed among young professionals: If your idea of "dressing up" comes from the club scene, you may be "dressing wrong" for business. Part of this has to do with the casual nature of college life, where spaghetti-strap tops and jammies and flip-flops are all perfectly normal attire. And sometimes when a person walks from the graduation stage to the corporate office, she fails to adjust her concept of "dressing up"—and shows up for work drop-dead gorgeous *for a date*. This is distracting at best and sends a very wrong message at worst.

If you don't know how to choose the right shoes for a suit, you have two solutions: Seek professional help, or take your clues from the most successful people around you. Who in the company is admired? Who is known to be a darling of senior management? Their subtle clues of dress might, and I do stress *might*, be good ones to follow.

I once had a wonderful career counselor who was assigned to work with executives. But she dressed like a secretary. I put up with it for a couple of months before I marched her across the street to one of the better women's haberdasheries in San Francisco and introduced her to Elizabeth. (I had prepped Elizabeth for this visit.) I handed my career counselor a large gift certificate. Problem solved.

Do not assume that your ideas of how to dress are universally admired. Test your ideas by discreetly asking someone you admire and trust for advice. Choose someone inside your organization, or at least in your industry.

And dress appropriately for your surroundings. Don't be the fashion plate in the shipping department, worried about breaking a nail.

INTERVIEW WITH ELLIE HALL ON WOMEN IN LEADERSHIP

[Ellie Hall is an independent organizational consultant based in Colorado and spent many years with the Center for Creative Leadership.]

Anytime you're in a leadership role you're under a microscope, and this is particularly true of women. It's really important to act the way you want to be thought about. If you want to be seen as a person who can be trusted, you have to act in a trustworthy way, fulfill your word, be known for fulfilling your word, and not get involved in gossip.

And like it or not, when you're an executive woman, people will read things into your actions; they'll insert motivations and implications that simply are not there. So you have to be aware all the time of what kind of perception you're creating versus the kind of perception you want to create.

How do you do this? You build feedback loops with people you trust, people who will be honest with you about how you're being perceived. Identify people who serve different roles for you. Some people you identify because they have a certain expertise and you can gain information from and bounce ideas off of them. I always say to pick one or two confidantes, people you can let your hair down and blow off steam with but who are highly trustworthy. Finally, you need someone higher up the organization, someone who is highly visible, to take an interest in you, to guide you, who can help make your career visible.

And, then there are those people who have power and you want to cultivate alliances with. They can have either position power or personal power; it doesn't matter. Do them favors, become known to them, have some value to them before you ask them to have any value to you. Don't just have relationships, but manage your relationships.

How do you get noticed? Women are so reluctant to showcase their achievements. You can't be afraid to point out to the right people what you've done. That's not to be a braggart, or to be arrogant, but to highlight projects you've worked on where your participation made a difference. And there really is such a thing as persona, an executive presence. If it's not natural to you, you have to learn it.

The other part is, because of stereotypes, women are often portrayed negatively if they approach work from an emotional standpoint. You never want to be dismissed for being openly emotional; you never want someone to say, "Oh, she's just being emotional." You can feel things, certainly, but the persona that you want to show others is being logical and living in your head. Get emotional behind closed doors when you're alone. Then, once you regain your composure, approach conflicts from a problem-solving standpoint and not from an interpersonal dilemma standpoint. It's not, "Can't we all get along," so much as, "How are we going to solve this problem?"

Some women feel that they have to take on the characteristics of a man to be successful or to be promoted, but that's really not the issue. *The most successful women are the ones who are themselves, but they've figured out how to relate to men.* You have to relate to the people who have the power and resources that you need to do your job, whether those people are men or women. You need to become comfortable around people with power and influence. But you can be feminine and be really successful, no question about it.

And for women headed to the top, there's a great deal of intentionality that goes into managing a career. Many women make the mistake of staying in traditionally female jobs such as H.R. or marketing or corporate communications, that sort of thing. And the research shows that one of the reasons that women don't get promoted is because they don't have general management experience, they don't have technical experience, and they don't have any profit-and-loss background. So if you really want to progress in an organization, you have to position yourself across the organization in various leadership roles.

That's the most important thing. You may want to head up a manufacturing or production function, then head up an IT group, then marketing, then distribution, looking for breadth as opposed to depth, so you're positioned for general management responsibilities. That's what men do, and they know to do it because they often have people looking out for them in their careers, helping them along. Women often don't have that, and they need to seek that out.

Here's another suggestion, and it is *hugely* important. As people progress in an organization, they tend to manage downward more and more; they spend most of their psychic energy managing their people. But as you progress in an organization, you really should shift your focus to managing outward, managing upward, and paying attention to all your stakeholders. You've got to gain those skills. Someone who is your peer one day can be your boss the next day, or can help *you* become the boss, so those relationships are critical. You need to work on forming alliances with people throughout the organization, even in cases where it's not obvious how their job could link to your job. If I'm the head of IT, I *need* to know the manager of finance.

My best advice for young people? Do some deep self-reflection. Get to know yourself. Because you have to have an overwhelming appetite to advance, to take on leadership roles in today's fast-paced and complex and stressful world. And if you don't have the appetite for it, that's okay; find what you do have the appetite for, and then go do that.

CHAPTER THREE

LIFELONG LEARNING IS REQUIRED FOR LIFELONG SUCCESS

> Fortune favors the prepared mind.
> —LOUIS PASTEUR

Know What You Need to Know <u>Before</u> You Need to Know It!

Lifelong learning used to be the province of medical doctors and scientists, but now it is a requirement for all careerists. What's different about fast-track people is that they *anticipate* the needs of their organizations. They are true lifelong learners, acquiring new skills on an ongoing basis with a strategy in mind: to have the skills they need for their next assignment before that assignment is even available to them.

Social scientists agree that we are living in a period of rapidly increasing complexity. Skillsets that used to get you into senior management now won't grant you success in middle management. Do you have a strategy to obtain the skills you will need to advance to the next level, to be ready to be promoted, and to be ready to perform if you are promoted? Perhaps we should forget about advancement and promotions for just a moment and talk about survival. Do you have a strategy to keep up with changes in your current field, or will change overtake you?

The days of leaving learning at the edge of the university campus are over. College and even graduate degrees are a smaller part of the formula for success than ever before. It is the ongoing, nimble, responsive and anticipatory learner who has a career advantage over others. Those who can design their own educational process, who teach themselves what they need to know, are known as autodidacts. We are entering the age of the autodidact.

Even if you have no degrees at all, you can be an autodidact. The only thing degrees confer is the imprimatur of the institutions that grant them. They indicate learning, *but it is the learning itself that is critical to success.*

Lifelong learning is a smorgasbord approach. You have to take it from wherever you can get it. Here are just a few of the sources:

- ☐ Internet. Search topics important in your business, taking care to sort out the garbage.

- ☐ Read several newspapers a day.

- ☐ Read all the trade publications for your field, trade, or discipline.

- ☐ Structure library learning on a topic of interest.

- ☐ Get advice from or even consulting with subject-matter experts.

- ☐ Develop in-house or external soft skills, such as leadership or EQ.

- ☐ Develop in-house or external hard skills, such as changes in GAAP, or Sarbanes-Oxley compliance or how to speak conversational French.

- ☐ Get vendor training or certification classes.

- ☐ Join a trade association and attend their training conferences and/or conventions, and subscribe to their member journals and newsletters.

- ☐ Attend management or executive retreats addressing a relevant topic or concern.

- ☐ Pursue executive development provided by the top business schools on topics of interest, such as globalism or developments in supply chain logistics or economic trends impacting an entire industry (generally considered post-MBA in content).

☐ Read your organization's in-house materials, such as manuals, product information, policies, and procedures, and discover secrets deeply hidden in obscure pages of its intranet.

☐ There are graduate and undergraduate degrees and certificates, offered by colleges and universities, coming in a complete range of formats: online (asynchronous or synchronous), distributed learning with intensives offered at various times of the year followed by periods of self-study, weekends or evening programs (cohort or noncohort), classes offered onsite at your employer's or offsite in a hotel, or more traditional residential programs with semesters or quarters and classes that begin with a bell.

☐ Evening and weekend courses are available from seminar companies in every major city.

☐ Enroll in Toastmaster's International to develop your speaking skills.

☐ Find and talk to people who know what you need to learn.

☐ What else? Be creative!

Do You Read the Newspaper?

Most young people today get their news from the Internet, but news sites contain approximately one twenty-fifth of the words in the news sections of a newspaper. So you may be missing a lot of information critical to your success.

Warren Buffet, the Oracle of Omaha, self-made billionaire, and at last count the second richest-man in the world, reads four newspapers a day to keep up on news and trends.

Howard Schultz, CEO of Starbucks, reads three newspapers a day with his morning coffee, and it seems to have helped him run a successful company.

I've been reading three or four newspapers a day for decades—so far to no effect.

Education has changed tremendously over the last twenty years, with an explosion of options never before available to working people. Now it is possible to pursue all kinds of educational attainment even while employed, and even if you have kids and a spouse, travel a lot, or have a big and active life outside of your job.

You can even obtain a Ph.D. while working full-time, through such wonderful, *accredited* options as Fielding Graduate University of Santa Barbara, California, and similar institutions offering a distributed learning model where you meet occasionally throughout the year and complete the rest of the program through distance learning. These types of programs didn't even exist until recently.

But it is not just whether you are learning constantly; it is also important *what* you are learning—and how relevant it is. This is why it is a *huge* career advantage to be an autodidact. You can obtain critical skills on the fly, as needed, and on short notice. You can obtain *the right skills* and *the needed skills* in a timely manner.

For example, are you active or passive when it comes to obtaining new skills? Do you reluctantly attend training classes as directed by your boss or by H.R. mandates, or do you seek out the training and skills development you need to advance to the next level? Are you willing to spend your own money to join critical trade organizations, attend association meetings, or obtain outside vendor training important for your own success and advancement? Most important of all, both to yourself and to your employer, do you anticipate your organization's *future* needs, obtain those skills on your own, and then offer them when your employer needs them?

Here's how H.R. professionals design a skillset intervention for an individual manager or for any class of workers:

1. Assess skillsets needed by the organization, especially skillsets needed because of some pending organizational change.

2. Assess skillsets possessed by the worker or class of workers.

3. Perform a gap analysis, that is, identify the difference between the skillset workers possess and the skillset the organization needs or wants them to possess.

4. Design a plan to bridge the gap. Determine where that bridge is too time-consuming, expensive, or difficult and then:

5. Design a plan to fire or reassign staff with the wrong skills and hire staff with the right ones.

Obviously, you need to do this yourself, *before* your boss or H.R. manager does it. As important as H.R. is, it is basically a reactive function. You need to be prescient, anticipatory, and ahead of the curve. Look at step number one above. Do you habitually do this?

Remember, you don't necessarily have to be expert to win an assignment! Exposure may be enough; knowing the jargon may be enough; a few lunches with a pal who has experience in the target

ASHER'S HIERARCHY OF LIFELONG LEARNING ACTUALIZATION Which of the following descriptions can be applied to you?	
6	Anticipator of skills needed by society as a whole
5	Anticipator of skills needed to advance to the next level in the organization
4	Active initiator of training and skills development inside and outside the company
3	Active initiator of training and skills development inside the company
2	Passive recipient of training, only when directed by others
1	Brain-dead moron who refuses to learn new skills

issue may be enough. But timing is everything. You need to act fast, before anyone else, because once H.R. gets ahold of it, a Ph.D. may be required.

One critical indicator of how committed you are to your own self-development is whether you will spend your own money on it. If your employer won't pay for you to belong to an organization, attend its meetings, or take a class outside your assignment area, *will you pay for it?* If not, you may just be a tourist in career land.

Note that this hierarchy reaches outside the organization to ask what skills society as a whole may need of its member-participants. This is in alignment with systems theory, current concerns of global sustainability, and a new accounting concept called the triple bottom line. The triple bottom line asks these three questions:

1. What is the financial outcome?

2. What is the social outcome?

3. What is the environmental outcome?

We are leaving an era of hedonism and me-first-ism and entering an era of renewed interest in boundary-spanning communitarian ethics, with a much bigger picture of what constitutes a community. Globalism can be viewed in different ways. The first wave was: Where in the world can I obtain more production or markets? The next wave is this: What are the impacts *anywhere in the world* of my decisions and actions?

Let us all hope that completing this shift does not come too late.

Are You a Dinosaur?

Things change, and if you don't change with them, you'll become a dinosaur. Even young people can be dinosaurs if they hang on to old ideas they inherited from their families or from growing up in a particular area of the country.

Hanging on to old skills, and refusing to learn new skills, can make you a dinosaur but so can hanging on to old concepts and old values.

Can you anticipate practices that are accepted today that will be abhorred about five minutes from now? Here's one: doing business in strip clubs. Here's another: exporting pollution to minority neighborhoods, rural areas, and foreign countries. And here's one more: companies that habitually abuse their employees will have serious retention problems as the pendulum swings back in favor of employees in the coming years. *Anticipate* these social changes, and you'll be ahead of other careerists and more valuable to your organization. Long-term career success is enhanced by being a bit of a futurist.

Notes from a Veteran Chief Technical Officer in the Silicon Valley

"We employ two types of people: People who just do their jobs—who got into this because when they were in college we were a hot sector—and people who live and breathe technology. I can tell the difference in a few moments. Unfortunately, the guy before me hired a bunch of people who are just putting in their time. He was from [a large company] and he bought credentials. I never buy credentials. I ask a guy what he does at night, and on weekends, and I listen really carefully to what he says about working on a problem. If he stops thinking about that problem at night, he's not my type of [employee]."

Learning from Other People

When you read a book, go to a website, take a class, or read a policies and procedures manual, you are learning information that was originally embodied in a live human being. Someone had the insight that was then recorded in some media, and as a student or investigator, you are accessing that information later.

Perhaps the best source of information is to go directly to those live human beings themselves, the ones who originally had the insights.

Part of lifelong learning is to learn from others who possess the information you need to obtain. When you read management books that talk about having a large network and having many mentors, what they mean is having direct access to people who can tell you how things work, how to solve problems, where to find help, and so on.

Be aware that sometimes the people with the most and best information are not necessarily people with position authority, with titles like head cashier, CTO, or director of H.R. Often it's people who have little or no authority who have the most *informational* power, like the A/P clerk who can tell you how to get your expense reports approved, the secretary who knows how to get a laptop requisition approved, or the person in every office who knows how to update software without losing your old files, and so on.

Overheard in the Bull and Bear

I overheard a guy yelling into his cell phone in the Bull and Bear bar in the Waldorf Astoria on Lexington in Manhattan: "Here's my promise to you: The minute I'm not learning every day, I'll submit my resignation. So that's not an issue."

Become a "People Collector"

Fast-track careerists prefer to get their information from living human beings. Fast-track careerists collect people the way some people collect stamps. They have, literally, hundreds of people whom they can call upon at any given time. And many of them do it systematically. They use contact management software, they write names and title or positions on the back of pictures, or they write down the names of every person at a meeting directly on the file or on the paperwork from that meeting.

Book learners—those who *primarily* get their information from static media—often *don't* become fast-track careerists, because the skills that are required to identify, access, and develop relationships

DIFFERENCES BETWEEN SUPERVISOR, MANAGER, EXECUTIVE, AND LEADER	
POSITION	DUTIES AND SKILLSET REQUIREMENTS
SUPERVISOR	Has direct technical expertise; can train others in it. Maintains appropriate social distance between self and those supervised. Has mental toughness to hire and fire. Can set clear expectations for direct reports. Has emotional maturity. Can resolve human conflicts. Can direct the activities of others.
MANAGER	All of the prior, plus: Monitors the activities of others. Can use data to make and support decisions. Understands a longer cycle of business, that is, can see seasons, product life cycles, budget cycles, and so on. Can execute strategy. Can achieve goals through subordinates; can delegate.
EXECUTIVE	All of the prior, plus: Can see strategy of the organization as a whole, can set the direction of the enterprise. Can see the organization in its external context. Can anticipate external threats, including broadly based industry and societal trends. Can achieve goals through subordinate structures, rather than personalities.
LEADER	All of the prior, plus: Can inspire. Can achieve efficiency of execution through inspiration rather than direction. Can call upon the power of ideas and moral persuasion, rather than the power of position. Represents the enterprise to society. Influences the practices of external others, be they competitors, suppliers, customers, or unrelated emulators.

with knowledgeable and powerful people are skills that tend to be rewarded, while information that is recorded in or on media is obsolete. As any teenage girl can tell you, the best way to get the most up-to-the-moment info is to call somebody.

Trade and professional association meetings are the best places to meet people who are leaders in their fields. Belong, and participate. Spend your own money to attend meetings if your employer won't send you. You are the one who benefits, and you'll be taking those benefits with you wherever you go.

You need a plan to develop the skillset necessary to deliver the mission of your *next* job, be it supervisor, manager, executive, or leader. Do you need to learn to give speeches, teach in a seminar format, analyze data, or even play golf? If so, it is *your responsibility* to obtain those skills in anticipation of your next promotion. For most organizations, it's skills first, promotion later—not the other way around.

Why People Earn Exactly What They Expect to Earn

For several decades I have been struck by the fact that people are mostly content with their salaries (not young people, certainly, but many people in the middle of their careers). Most people earn about what they expected to earn or are about as happy with their incomes as they expected to be. So why is this?

This is true for the same reason that you find things in the last place you looked. You find things in the last place you looked because once you've found something, you no longer need to look for it. Using the exact same human logic, once you earn what you expected to earn, or earn enough to meet your needs, you no longer will switch jobs or careers in order to earn more.

You are content.

So my suggestion to you is rather simple: Be less satisfied. Decide you are worth more. *Expect to earn more.* And whatever number you choose, within reason, that is the number you will earn.

"I Quit!" "You're Hired!"

Vannetta S. was a star performer in technical customer support for a large multinational. She had a couple of favorite sayings: "Always be fabulous!" and "Look good, do good, be good." Her boss thought he'd found a gold mine when he hired her. She inspired others in the department, including people above her. She earned so many raises that she was bumped to the top of her pay grade, earning the maximum that H.R. rules allowed. But her boss had hiring authority. So Vannetta and the boss made a pact. On Friday evening, as she headed out of the office, she said, "I quit." And on Monday morning when she came in he said, "You're rehired." He processed the paperwork to record her separation, and then he rehired her with a jump in grade. For six months they thought they'd get busted by H.R., but they never heard a word about it. Fabulous!

Does It Pay to Let Your Employer Pay for Your Ongoing Education?

One of the problems with letting your employer pay for your continuing education is that they often don't want to pay you more for it *later*. Before you get too excited about education benefits, check the details. Some don't pay up front; they only reimburse you for courses you have finished. Many won't pay for books, fees, and other directly related expenses. There may be restrictions on topics (for example, the course or degree program must be related to your current assignment). And worst of all, many include a pay-back clause if you leave the company before a specified time after you complete the course of study. So your night MBA "paid for" by a company might chain you to that company for five years after graduation. That's no problem if your compensation is increasing and your advancement is progressing, but five years of career stagnation is not worth any amount of education benefit.

All too often your only reward for completing a degree while with the same employer is a congratulations and a greeting card. That's a pretty low return on your investment of time and energy, regardless of who pays the tuition.

One way to deal with this is to set clear expectations with your employer that you will get a boost in pay and a new assignment upon completing a certification or degree program.

Interview with a Secretary Promoted to Management

"I was like the last person you would ever think would be promoted. I was a fifty-year-old male secretary who'd been with the organization for twenty years. I was the only gay guy in the department. I was the only one in the department without a college degree. And although I got along with everyone, absolutely no one thought of me as 'high potential.'

"On top of all that, this place was really old school. They still had us make the coffee and bring the doughnuts, stuff that quit happening in the corporate world twenty years ago. But this was [a health and human services department for a major city]. There was an iron curtain between support staff and professional staff. No one had ever crossed over before.

"You might ask how I came to be in this position, but everyone develops at their own pace. I had some things of my own to work out, and the job wasn't my top priority for a long time. But then one day it was. So I decided to go to night school. I signed up for a degree completion program that would take two years. It was the smartest thing I ever did. But I asked myself, how am I ever going to get them to take me seriously at work? How am I going to get credit for this degree? And then I had a flash of brilliance.

"I am the one who does all the holiday designs for our department. You want Halloween? You want Fourth of July? That's me. So I decided to make an installation out of my education. I put up a big banner behind my desk, 'Robert is going to college!' It was corny, I know, but it started the conversation. I left that up way too long, a couple of months at least, and then I replaced it with a calendar. The calendar was a countdown to my graduation. 'Months until Robert graduates from college.' I left that up for a month or two, until I finally revealed my true intent. I replaced the headline to read 'Months until Robert is no longer a secretary!'

"I think it was nonthreatening by then. If I'd started out with that, maybe I'd have gotten some criticism. I don't know. Also, by then, I had almost six months of success in the program. People could see it was not a fad. They could see I was going to make it.

"In the final year, I changed it to be 'Days until Robert is no longer a secretary!' I wrote the titles of my papers on the calendar, and people could see that they were related to our mission. Every couple of months I redesigned the thing. Finally, I started putting a big X on each day that brought me closer to graduation. And then a really weird thing started to happen. People began to ask me what kind of assignment I wanted. Everyone in the office was looking for a job for me.

"Even my boss, who made it no secret that she didn't want me to leave, got the hint. She started referring me for jobs in our organization, and other jobs city-wide. I got a job across the hall as a case manager. I actually got to write the position requisition for my replacement. That was a sweet moment.

"Now I'm signed up for an evening master's degree. I know I can do more. I probably won't do the calendar thing again, but it was absolutely the key to my promotion."

When a Raise Is an Insult

While working for a government agency in California, Maureen D. received a 4 percent management-grade raise, and in the same year a 7 percent merit raise for outstanding performance. H.R. processed the 7 percent raise at 3 percent. When she inquired about the "mistake" they told her that she had already gotten a 4 percent raise. She asked to see the policy that allowed this interpretation of a merit raise, basically robbing her of part of her deserved reward. "You're looking at it," the H.R. rep replied. Maureen protested formally, but the interpretation stuck, an excellent example of the power of TNTWWDIAH (That's Not the Way We Do It Around Here).

INTERVIEW WITH
AN AUTODIDACT

My employer has its own football team, its own police force, and its own nuclear reactor. Only a truly elite university has such a combination of business units, and I work for one of the most elite of all. Let's just say you can smell salt water from my office.

I'm very fortunate to have the perfect job. I work with really smart people in scientific computing for a research institute supporting multiple universities. I work directly with the faculty, and I supervise doctoral candidates and post-docs, even though I myself don't have any advanced degree.

But one thing I do have is the ability to teach myself whatever it is I need to know. Since we are developing new scientific software, there's no such thing as a certification program for what we do. You have to figure it out as you go. It's like running a marathon, with hurdles, only you have to build the hurdles yourself while you keep running.

Since I don't have a Ph.D., you might say I've had to do a little extra to prove myself. And the faculty here can be very demanding. One of the things that has allowed me to stay ahead of them is that I am willing to slog through the fine print. They might glance at a tech manual or spec sheet, but I'll read every word and double check every function. They don't have the patience for that. My job is to create a bridge between something they invent and the scientists who will eventually use that product. A lot of times they don't even know what it will do yet, and I have to commercialize it for release.

I've gotten four promotions and eight pay raises in just six years, which most people would consider impossible in a university setting. I earn six figures in an industry that is notorious for underpaying talent. Since I knew you were going to be calling, I've had time to think about how that came about. First of all, it was not an accident. Luck matters, sure, but my success was built on three things.

First of all, I am perfectly happy to be continually learning. A lot of people talk about continuing education, but I'm talking about con-tin*ual* education. I like it. It's the opposite of hard for me. So this is the foundation of my success.

The walls of my success, to torture a metaphor, are hard work. I basically work if I am awake. I'm the go-to guy. I'm the guy you know will deliver.

And the roof of my success, the thing that keeps out the weather and protects what I have built, is my relationships with faculty. I live in a soft-money world. Projects form and dissolve, and so you are always looking for an assignment. If faculty know you and like you, this works out fine. But if you piss off the faculty, you get fired by not picking up a new assignment.

Here's my career path: I got hired as a programmer analyst II, a nice hard-money assignment with security forever. The woman who hired me liked me. "Look," she said, "You can't get promoted in this unit. You've got to look around for something better." It was great advice.

So with her blessing, I started interviewing all over campus, looking for something better. I picked up a PA III slot in another department, still hard money, still a job for life. The guy I supposedly worked for didn't like to work very much, so I basically did his job for him. He was ROTJ [retired on the job], and I was emailing the department head in the middle of the night and responding to his job queries within a few minutes no matter when he pinged me. A cash-flow squeeze hit the whole university, and they actually gave my boss the axe. I did two jobs for a year before I got the promotion. That's basically how you get promoted here: You do two jobs for awhile, and if you succeed, they'll make it official. Eventually. So then I was a PA IV.

Then I switched over to the research institute as a PA V. The only way to get ahead, is to keep switching departments and extracting at least a 10 or 15 percent raise each time. You can't get ahead on the seniority system. That's for the ghouls, you know, the walking brain dead.

About this time I got called in by H.R., and they said, "You can't have any more raises. Somehow you've already had more raises than are allowed by the system." I said, "Well, is there any circumstance under which I might be allowed another raise before twelve months from now?" "Yes," she said, "If you got a written offer from another employer, you might qualify for a retention adjustment."

Well, thank you very much. Duh. So I put myself on the market, and got a written offer that I had no intention of accepting. I took it to my boss and said, "Hey, I like the university. I really like you guys. So, what can we do?" He got it approved, and that's how I got my current grade. They had to make up a title for me. So I am a software scientist II. The only one in the system. It's just a made-up title.

My advice? Three things: Get off your butt and learn what you need to know before anyone else does. Become known as a problem solver and, frankly, that means deliver the hard work. Slackers don't advance very far. And make sure that lots of people know you're a problem solver, not just the boss you have today but anyone who might be your boss in the future. Finally—and it took me some time to get how important this is—learn how to say no. Have a can-do attitude, but don't be a yes man. When something's not a winner, you have to learn to say, without whining, "No, I don't want to do that. That's not a good idea," or "That's not possible." I don't tell a boss what to do, really, but I lay out the options and help the manager make smarter decisions about work flow. Believe me, it is better to say no to something than to fail at it. Hard work, staying up with the learning, and being honest have worked pretty well for me.

CHAPTER FOUR

ALL BUSINESS IS SALES

Business Is Great! People Are Wonderful!

All of business is sales. If you don't think you are in sales, you are simply mistaken. Accountants are in sales. Engineers are in sales. If you're not selling your company, you're selling yourself. If you're not selling yourself, you're selling your ideas. If you are on a team, the team will take direction from the person who best sells her ideas to the others. If you are being observed by senior management for promotion, it is not the best performer who is promoted but the performer who is *perceived* to be the best. Your ability to sell your skills and your potential determines how you are perceived and creates your long-term career success.

As mentioned, accountants who test out on personality tests as highly confident are ranked more highly skilled by their bosses and their peers than accountants who test out highly knowledgeable on accounting. In other words, it may in fact be more important to *appear* to know what you are doing than to *actually* know what you are doing.

One of my first jobs was selling advertising, and I have to admit I was not very good at it. After a day of dragging around my magazine samples and my spiel, I returned to the sales office discouraged and beaten. "How'd it go?" my manager asked. "Lousy," I said. "Nobody wants to buy advertising in our silly little tourist magazine."

"No," he said, "Nobody wants to buy *you*. *You* are no fun. *You* are not a good time. *You* are the picture of a bad hair day, my boy. Whenever anyone asks you how business is going, you say 'Incredible!' or 'Unbelievable!' You don't have to say 'Incredibly bad!' Always tell the truth, but know when to shut up. So, business is incredible! Everything is looking up! It's great to be in business! Business is great! People are wonderful!"

I took his lesson to heart and, although he fired me, I became the number one salesperson in the country for my next employer, a company with over four hundred offices, coast to coast. Things were looking up! Business was great! And people *are* wonderful!

What goes into being a salesperson? Six things really matter:

1. Attitude

2. The ability to think like someone else

3. The ability to prepare for a meeting

4. Persistence

5. The ability to overcome objections to get to "yes"

6. Creativity of message

Attitude

Are you somebody other people want to be around? Or are you negative, nasty, gossipy, and whiney like a bad baby?

I once had an associate in a career-counseling office who was very talented at her job, very smart, had every credential, but was simply one of the most negative people I've ever known personally. She came in the door complaining about how far away from the building she had to park, about the weather, about something she saw on the morning news, about her work load, and how her cat puked on her shoes. And all of that was before she got into her own office. *Nobody wanted to talk to her, ever.* People ran from her. I wouldn't go to lunch with this woman, much less advance her for promotion.

People who are negative, who complain constantly, are not going to get promoted. Unfortunately, a lot of people who have been passed over for promotions become bitter about it and let it show, which pretty much ensures that their career advancement with that organization is over.

You *can* change your attitude. Just stop complaining. Stop whining. Keep your negativity to yourself. Bite your tongue if you have to!

Zig Ziglar, one of the greatest sales trainers in the world, advocates repeating a list of affirmations into the mirror each morning. You can literally fool your subconscious into believing in a new you. Slap a big smile on your face, look yourself in the eye, and say:

- ☐ I am in a great mood!

- ☐ I am going to have a great day!

- ☐ I am in charge of my feelings!

- ☐ I can choose how I react today!

This technique really works, and the more you stick with it the *more* it works. Even if you can't change your mood all the time, you may be able to use this technique to psyche yourself up for critical meetings and presentations. You may not be able to silence that inner voice of negativity, but at the very least, it can help you keep those negative thoughts to yourself.

Heather G. Gets Passed Over and Then Up

Heather G. was the young assistant director of H.R. for a major law firm based on the West Coast. When the director of H.R. gave notice, she applied for the position. She was frustrated to learn that the senior partners wanted to hire from outside, to "look for some new talent." Heather was told she was a finalist, but she felt it was just a courtesy because some of the partners thought she was just too young. When she was proved right after they hired an H.R. veteran from a large law firm across the country, Heather decided that she was going to start a secret search for another position. She knew she needed a good reference, so she was pleasant, continued to contribute good ideas and never let herself act hurt or resentful around her new boss or the partners.

The new H.R. director approached the managing partners and suggested that they create a new position for her—chief administrative officer. She identified a series of operational changes she wanted to implement in her new role that would improve efficiencies and reduce costs. Her ideas spanned billing, rainmaking, risk reduction, IT, and information flows. In short, she wanted a line position, directly under the senior partners, with the authority to impact P&L. The partners agreed. The new H.R. director was appointed the CAO, and her first act was to promote Heather to be director of H.R. The CAO told Heather, "I was so impressed with your professionalism, because I knew that you had been a finalist for the position, and the quality of your ideas is great. So take the assignment and show me what you can do with it."

Gossip

By the way, gossip is almost always negative, distracting, and can be dangerous. Listen to gossip, if you have to, but don't traffic in it. Business is great! People are wonderful! Remember, if you stick a knife in a rival's back, your fingerprints will be all over the murder weapon.

Besides, don't you have a lot to be grateful for? Make a list. Here's mine for today:

I live in a great country.

I have great friends.

I love my job 99 percent of the time.

My dog loves me.

I have a cool cat.

My parents are wonderful.

I had an idyllic childhood.

I'm wealthy.

My wife is awesome.

I'm better looking every day.

I could think the opposite of any one of these if I wanted to, but I don't. Have an attitude of gratitude, and people will be drawn to you.

The Ability to Think Like Someone Else

Can you think like someone else? This is one of the hallmarks of emotional maturity, and it's also the secret weapon of all top sales professionals. If you want to influence others, you must first understand their thoughts, feelings, and motivations.

In organizations of all types, the number-one concern of all human beings is: WIFM (What's in it for me?). What can you offer to me personally, to my department, to my function or mission, to my organization as a whole? You need to be able to understand what someone else *wants* in order to motivate them.

Sure, some people are motivated by altruism. They may believe that what's good for the shareholders—or for the planet—is good for themselves, but more people are motivated by what's simply good for them. The more accurately you can understand what someone else wants, the more successfully you can influence and motivate them.

That's selling—being cognizant of others' needs. Selling isn't bad. It is simply how ideas are spread from one person to another.

Selling is increasingly important in contemporary organizations because of two trends: First, organizations are flatter and flatter, and ideas can come from any direction. Ideas don't flow from the top down any more; they flow up, down, and sideways. You may not have structural authority over those whom you need to influence. You may have to influence a boss, over whom you have no structural authority at all, or a matrix-function partner where without buy-in, you will not obtain cooperation, so business structures themselves require more selling.

Second, we are becoming a knowledge-based society rather than a production society. The content of business is different. Information requires selling in a way that production does not. If you are supervising someone doing labor, authority is about all you need. If you are trying to develop a more competitive service product, you need to influence others in an entirely different way. You need to *persuade* them.

So before you attempt to influence someone, spend some time looking at the world from their point of view. Try on their mindset. Understand where they're coming from. How will your suggestion impact their world? You better know that first, before you structure your appeal to them.

Top salespeople can make one presentation to the CFO (money), another to engineering (technology), and another to end users (ease and convenience). They'll mention boating to the company officer who boats, golfing to the woman who golfs, sports to that guy who loves the local sports franchise, and kids to the new moms and dads. They decorate their ideas in the package most attractive to the buyer, not the seller.

Remember that trends are predictable but people are unique. The CFO may care more about the environment than he does the shareholders, and a female account exec may care more about sports than any man you've ever met, or a warehouse manager may care more about his kids than he does his career. So while you are trying to generalize, don't forget to customize!

Next time you are trying to sell an idea, consider your audience systematically. What do they want? What do they fear? How can you present your information in a format that is most relevant to the listener, one that maximizes perceptions of reward and minimizes perceptions of risk? That is how you sell ideas.

Don't Know Much about Horse Breeding

Carlton W. had a meeting with the executive team of a horse breeding association to pitch them for software design. They wanted a way to record the lineage of every horse in the history of racing, the performance of every horse in every race relative to all the specific other horses in each race, and the cash value of the winnings, adjusted for inflation. The goal was to make this available to members on their website.

Carlton had competitors, at least two that he knew of. One competitor was a large organization with a good name. The other was a small shop like Carlton's. Carlton had two kids in private schools, and he needed this assignment badly. Going last, he would have to stand out from both of his competitors or walk home without a contract.

When he went in to deliver his pitch, he said very little about technology, dismissing the issue by saying, "The technology that we will use to do this is well established." This was only partially true. But he didn't think these horse breeders would find the actual current status of software design to be very interesting. They were going to be interested in horses, horse racing, and horse people. "The important thing is to have someone design this software who understands genealogy and the business of horse breeding and horse racing." Then he proceeded to tell them everything he had learned in preparation for the meeting, that horses were more valuable as breeders than racers, that the best racers in the world were kept off the tracks due to fear of injuries, and that changes in tax laws had recently had a major impact on horse ranching practices. He even knew the blood lines of a couple of famous horses.

Technologically, Carlton was the weakest of the three presenters. But Carlton wasn't selling technology; he was selling ideas. He got the contract.

How to Prepare for a Meeting

I work with corporate officers in transition who earn from $200,000 to several million a year. When they go into an interview, there's a lot of money on the table, and they function in sudden-death overtime; if you make a mistake, there isn't another opportunity to come back and even the series. These interviews typically involve several people, a headhunter (who is more worried about his reputation than this particular placement and *hates* surprises), a CEO or president (who needs the right help right now), and an H.R. officer (who will make a mark on the meeting somehow to justify being invited).

Here's how we prepare for meetings: We establish the format, length, and purpose of the meeting. Is it a screening meeting, a decision meeting, or a salary negotiation? Is it a series of one-on-ones, a group, structured or unstructured, and will there be a meal or a social setting? We discuss our candidate's likely status in the search process. What are her strengths, and how will they attack her weaknesses? We prepare opposition points; how can we instill doubt about her competition? We prepare success stories, and a series of specific points that the candidate will make as the meeting progresses. We spend time on branding and differentiation in preparation for this series of questions: Why is she the right person, why is this the right job for her, and why now? We discuss each person's motivations, concerns, and desires at some length. What will this person care about, and what do you think his role is going to be, and what might he say? Then we model various scenarios for how the meeting might go.

Most important of all, we role play each person. The CEO is going to say this; what will your response be? The H.R. person is going to say this or that; how will you respond? They are going to go after this weakness in your background; what will you say? We make notes and audio tapes of this preparation. Then, just before the meeting, the candidate will close her eyes and do a walkthrough of all the possibilities.

Of course you can overprepare for any event, to the extent that if you go off script you are in trouble. In a live event like a meeting involving several people, you can only anticipate about half of what's going to happen. But if you can anticipate and prepare for the concerns of the key players in the room, you can look pretty smart. This approach can be used for all types of pitch meetings as well. Whether you are going to pitch a client for business or pitch a boss for a promotion, walking through the motivations of the other participants and modeling your responses can improve your performance tremendously. When there's a lot of money on the table, it just makes sense.

At the Corporate Retreat: Interview with Wilson S.

"Last week I went to my first corporate retreat. We got off a plane in Chicago and went a few miles by bus to a world you would never believe was so close to a major city. There's this rustic lodge, the furniture was all handmade, held together with horseshoes, and similar hokey stuff, with massive fireplaces in every room. Right out of a movie. Just outside the door were these trout streams, which I think were totally artificial. The fish were like pets. Anyway, it didn't matter. We were there to consider a struggling software integration company suffering from offshore competition. Our assignment was to come back with recommendations to get it back on track again and profitable. The company had expertise in a couple of major platforms, but they were stuck in a rut of doing a lot of small jobs involving subsystems, plus they had both top- and bottom-line problems and staffing issues. Most of us thought this was a subsidiary, but we found out later it was an acquisition target.

"We broke up into four teams, three different times, and we re-sorted the teams each time, creating twelve total configurations. Each team picked a leader, and the leader made each presentation back to the rest of the group. It was like twelve episodes of *The Apprentice* in one three-day intensive. We worked every day from eight a.m. to one or two o'clock in the morning.

"One weird thing was that there was an open bar all the time. Food, energy drinks, I could understand, but I didn't get the bar. Then I had an 'aha' moment. They were studying us as much as they were interested in our scenario modeling for this acquisition. They were seeing who was chosen leader, how good the ideas were, and who had too much to drink and maybe had a drinking problem. We were just as much guinea pigs as we were the scientists! I did pretty well.

I managed to get chosen leader each time. Only some of our ideas were advanced into the final plans, but we did okay. I heard already that I got noticed."

Persistence

Studies of sales professionals consistently find one big difference between successful salespeople and sales duds: the successful sales person tries more times than the dud.

In fact, this is one of the *only* surefire differences between successful sales people and unsuccessful sales people. Salespeople can be introverted, unattractive, inarticulate, have a bad sales technique, and have a bad product. But if they just get out there and try more times than other people, they can be truly successful.

What does this mean in an organizational setting?

It does *not* mean that you stalk your superiors or pester them over and over again for a raise, for a promotion, or to pitch the same old tired ideas. It means that if you want to sell your ideas you keep trying. You keep speaking up in meetings. You keep going out to lunch with people from the shipping department to try to resolve your shipping problems. You keep trying to reach the European sales rep who does not seem to have a cell phone. You try a different rationale when the first one fails. You try a different channel to find the real decision-maker. You keep trying. You are persistent.

And you vary your medium of delivery. Advertising research shows that people need multiple impressions *from multiple media* before they will buy. They need to see the ad on TV, read the ad in the paper, and hear about the product by word of mouth. Multiple exposures are powerful, and multiple exposures via multiple media are very, very powerful. So you bring up an idea in a staff meeting, you bring it up again at a dinner with peers, you sneak a slide about the idea into a presentation about something else, you have an intermediary tell your decision-maker that *they* think it is a good idea, you point out that the idea was originally suggested by a client, and so on.

If your ideas are important, try to get them heard, and keep trying, but not the same way each time. Present them in many different ways and in many different venues and through many different voices.

The Ability to Overcome Objections to Get to "Yes"

When someone objects to your ideas, it does not mean that they are not good ideas, and it certainly doesn't mean that they won't adopt them. Objections are like a verbal clearing of the throat. They are a form of sparring. *If you don't care about your idea enough to overcome a few objections, even you don't think it's a very good idea!*

There are certain objections that are so common they have their own acronyms:

- ☐ NIH: Not invented here.

- ☐ WTTA: We tried that already.

- ☐ TTWWDIAH: That's the way we do it around here.

- ☐ TNTWWDIAH: That's not the way we do it around here.

In fact, objections are good. If you're not hearing objections, it means your idea is not truly being considered. Conversely, it is only when you do hear objections that you can have any faith that your idea is gaining an audience and that you have a chance of advancing toward agreement.

Anticipating objections is part of making any presentation of ideas. Be ready with responses:

- ☐ To NIH: But that's not a rational reason for not trying it out if it will help us reach our goal.

- ☐ To WTTA: Yes, but the conditions that made it fail last time are not in play this time.

- ☐ To TTWWDIAH/TNTWWDIAH: Same as NIH.

Some version of turf war is often the root of many objections. If someone says, "If you do this, I will lose power, prestige, resources, or opportunity," then you have to either deny that this is true, and provide some evidence, or hold the speaker to a higher authority, such as that it is good for the department, the mission, the organization, or the planet.

Remember, stop and consider your listeners' points of view. You have to establish benefits *for them* and risk reduction *for them*. This can be a challenge with multiple constituencies in the room, but this is what sales is all about.

Interestingly enough, objections are not always logical. They are a linguistic device, rather than a logical framework. If you think of a conversation as a tennis match, an objection is a volley. *Anything* you say in response to an objection is a return volley. Very sophisticated salespeople know that you can agree with any objection, and in the majority of cases it will simply fade away as the conversation continues. Here is an example:

Boss: "That's the stupidest idea you've ever had!"

You: "Well, I see how at first glance it looks stupid."

(Weird, uncomfortable silence.)

Boss: "But, as you think about it, there is a possibility. . . ."

Don't worry about the logic of objections so much as having the conversation continue. In a group, this technique does not work, as someone will jump into any gap with *their* ideas, but one-on-one it can be a powerful secret weapon.

By the way, never hang onto your idea so tightly that you cannot let it become a live thing in the room. The surest way to get shot down is to not let others tack amendments and contingencies onto your idea, so don't jealously hang onto *your* version of it. If you let others contribute, they will begin to own your idea, and they will be much more likely to back some version of it. Remember, the most talented subordinates can give ideas to their boss and get the boss to think she came up with them first.

Creativity of Message

How many different ways can you say the same thing? If your message is not finding a ready audience, you need to get creative as many times as necessary. Keep changing your message—while keeping the same point. Miller Lite uses two slogans, and two slogans are better than one: Tastes great! Less filling! What's their point? Buy Miller Lite. Dodge often advertises to two audiences in the same ad, targeting women with safety and men with power. A talented trial lawyer can give five objections to anything a witness might say. The more objections she can lay out, the more chances that the judge will buy into at least one of them.

So if your boss rejects your idea, you may need to *restate it* and *reposition it* several times to improve its chances of being accepted. When you go in to ask for a raise, the more different rationales you can provide for why you ought to get this raise, and why you ought to get it now, the better your chances. If you want a promotion, multiple rationales can help your boss see you as the right choice.

Want to think more creatively? Practice by adopting differing points of view. Be nimble. Use more than one rationale. Try arguing the other side of your own position to understand your opponent better. Take the example of a politician, speaking before the public. He may have to answer a question without knowing the point of view of the questioner or the mood of the crowd. Here's an example in caricature, if you can imagine a Louisiana politician from an earlier era:

Q: "Sir, what is your position on alcohol?"

A: "My friend, if by alcohol you mean that scourge upon our families, that takes our young men away from their children in the evenings, when they need their daddies the most, and takes the food from the very mouths of their very own babies and is the root cause of so much violence in our homes and so many deadly and near-deadly car wrecks, if, my friends, you mean that alcohol that robs the mother of money for the most basic of necessities in her home and that causes so many, many lost days of work and ravages our economy in both subtle and not-so-subtle ways, that evil that wrecks the health of many, some of our most productive citizens, in their prime, and drives up the cost of medicine for all of us, then I am absolutely against it.

"But if by alcohol you mean that sacrament used in our sacred Catholic churches or that blessing by which every new bride and groom is toasted, and if you mean the many beverages over which good friends convene, and if you mean that civil sharing of the God-given product of the fruit and the grain that seals many a good business deal and that product, fairly taxed, that brings in so much money for our community coffers, that supports so much good works through this revenue, and if, my friends, by alcohol you mean that magical elixir that allows the shy man to ask the woman to dance and that allows the shy woman to say yes, she'd enjoy a dance, and thereby ensures the success of our community's celebrations and indeed, the continuation of our human race, then I am wholly for it!"

Obviously this is an over-the-top example, but it's an effective demonstration of creativity of message. Huey Long was elected governor of Louisiana, and then U.S. senator, on exactly this type of bombast. This type of rhetoric, black but white, yes *and* no, is demonstrated often in politics, including by the current occupant of the state house, no matter when you may read this sentence and no matter in which country you reside.

Try arguing the other side of any position you hold dear. It will help you become more creative with your message. It will help you foresee objections, help you better understand how to think like an "other," and be better able to persuade others who think differently than you. The point is this: If you will become better able to be creative with your message, you will become better at selling the side you really care about.

By the way, creativity is the one trait most common to top executives. They may be short or tall, glib or thoughtful, male or female, but they almost all test out high on creativity scales.

Sales Will Not Solve All Problems

In summary, it doesn't matter whether your environment is nonprofit, government, education, or the business world, sales gets your ideas an audience. An executive who cannot sell her ideas will not be an executive for long. In the end, however, sales are only a conveyor. It is a very necessary conveyor, but the product, idea, or person being conveyed must have value. If it does not, no amount of sales talent can disguise it forever. As Abraham Lincoln said, "You can fool all the people some of the time, and some of the people all the time, but you cannot fool all the people all the time."

Sales techniques are some of the most important of executive tools, but don't rely on them to cover up for poor ideas or poor performance.

The Dinosaur Zoo

Frattus despicabilus. The frat boy who objectifies all women as potential sexual partners and doesn't see them as real people. This beast's consciousness is so primitive he often cannot recognize his own image in a mirror.

Technos ludditus. The late adopter who is always trying to find someone else to set up his computer or update his software or program his phone or his music device. This arcane species often thinks his inability is "cute," but watch closely and you can see his coworkers roll their eyes.

Graspus supporticus. The person still looking around for the support staff who long ago disappeared from flat organizational charts. They often can't do mail merge or manage a simple contact database. It's pathetic, but it's curious to watch it try to do its own work.

Girlievoice eyebatticus. This creature wraps her male counterparts around her little finger with a hint of possible sexual favors. Very interesting to see in the mating dance with a *Frattus despicabilus*, a dance which can go on for years to the disgust of all in the general vicinity.

Yellus bellicosus. The petty straw boss who abuses subordinates with verbal tirades. He often loses all talent from subordinate teams and eventually gets written up for anger management classes—a rare species in the modern world, but certainly dangerous and to be avoided.

INTERVIEW WITH A HOTEL DEPARTMENT HEAD RE GOSSIP

I paid my way through college by being a food server at an expensive restaurant. I never studied at night anyway, and while other students were spending money in clubs, I was earning enough so that I graduated with zero debt. So it was natural for me to get my master's degree in hotel and hospitality management. Now I'm about halfway to making [hotel] general manager for a major property.

There are two keys to success here: First, you have to take every training offered, no matter how dumb and how off topic. If they have a training program on how to answer the phone, I go. And second, you have to rotate through all the departments to make G.M. There is no formal rotation program, so you have to talk your way into new departments. Luckily, there's a lot of turnover in hotels, and a lot of that turnover is sudden. People quit by walking toward the door. I've been functional head twice already—rooms, and food and beverage.

Now I have what some people consider the worst rotation: housekeeping. Personally, I like it. It's everything important about hotels—service, operations, staffing, cost control. And you get to live on property. Oh, and you have to speak Spanish. I took Spanish in high school *and* college, or I couldn't even do this job.

One thing I have to worry about in my career is gossip. This is a very people-oriented business, and people gossip. The worst is rooms division. Those people at the desk have way too much time on their hands. Our G.M. gets a lot of her daily information from the front-desk people. So one key to my success is managing gossip.

This might sound radical, but I have a preemptive program for gossip. Every day I imagine what someone *might* be saying about me, and I try to manage the message. Believe it or not, I got this from a business communications class in college! There're two sides to this, positive gossip and negative gossip. Negative gossip is the more important as it is by far the most powerful.

If someone has a negative experience, they tell six to ten other people, and those people tell even more people, and worst of all, the story tends to get amplified. So maybe the problem started out that your guest tripped over an extension cord and stubbed his toe in the lobby. And by the time it gets to the G.M., a guest was *intentionally* tripped by a housekeeper, had a compound fracture, was hauled off in an ambulance, and we've already heard from his lawyer!

Let me give you an example from today. A guy complains because the glass in his room wasn't clean. He said it looked like someone had brushed his teeth in it. Worst of all, he had drunk out of it before he noticed. So he's hot. The guy had found a way to complain twice at the front desk before I came on duty. So I go to his room, apologize profusely, and take him a couple of drink coupons and a bag of cookies. I get him some fresh glasses, which, miraculously, no one had thought to do yet. He calms down. But he's not my real problem, is he? My real problem is the gossip.

I had to analyze the problem, isolate the problem, and turn it into a success story. I already knew what the problem was, really. Alka Seltzer. Alka Seltzer leaves a residue that our dishwasher doesn't remove entirely. So I immediately fire off an email to the G.M. about how I had resolved this big guest complaint and that I had identified the problem, posted a big warning sign in English and Spanish about checking all the glasses, and personally checked all the other glasses on that floor and hadn't found another one that was less than crystal clean. Then I went to the front desk and casually dropped the whole Alka Seltzer story.

If I had not *proactively managed the gossip*, you can only imagine what they'd all be saying: that we had staff who put dirty glasses back in rooms, or something worse.

I manage the positive gossip, too. I try to make a point of telling the front-desk people all my hero stories. When one of my staff does an above and beyond, I don't let an hour pass before I drop the story on the front-desk people. It's like a telephone line straight into the

G.M.'s office. It could hurt me, but instead I use it to my advantage every day.

My advice to anyone trying to get ahead is not to ignore gossip—like some of the management books recommend—but to manage it in your favor. In every company there're a few people who are just like the send-all feature in email. You tell them and you've told everybody. Manage the message. That's what I say.

CHAPTER FIVE

YOU
ASCENSION PLAN,
NEED AN
BUT . . .

What Is an Ascension Plan?

Companies have succession plans for key officers. Companies plan *in advance* how they will replace key personnel. Some parts of these plans are secret, and some are common knowledge. If the CFO is killed in a plane wreck or develops a cocaine habit, the H.R. chief and the rest of the executive team need a plan to cover that position. If the president gets deposed, they know how they would cover his functions until they could decide on a new president. This is critical for institutional continuity.

Likewise, a careerist ought to have an **ascension plan** for career continuity, a plan for how she will ascend in her career. Just as in a succession plan, sometimes an ascension plan may be highly speculative and subject to complex contingencies and certainly ought to be open to constant revision. ***But I never met a fast-track careerist who didn't have a plan to create her next opportunity.***

These plans do not just include wish lists of appointments and time lines for advancement. They also include honest assessments of the skillsets and experiential development that will be necessary to be awarded advancement, and necessary to perform in the position once promoted!

Ascension plans also often have event triggers. Time is the most common event trigger: "If I am not promoted in this department within two years, I am going to aggressively seek a new assignment or even a new job." But event triggers can also be accomplishments or other milestones. Here are some examples:

- ☐ "I will be expecting a promotion when I finish my evening MBA program, and I will try to make sure that happens even though I am going to be busy as heck getting the program done while I manage my job at the same time."

- ☐ "I'm going to put myself on the line for Ruby's job when she retires, and if I don't get it, I'm going to leave. That's going to be my sign regarding my future with this organization."

- ☐ "I want a new assignment by my thirtieth birthday or else I'm just going to join a nunnery and give up on the whole thing."

Any reasonable plan needs both a goal and a time line, and you need to respect career paths. A tech-support clerk is not going to be named a company officer. A brand new attorney is not going to be promoted to be general counsel. And in a lot of companies, staff positions do not lead to the top job, only line positions do. So if you're in H.R. with no business-unit leadership and no P&L background, you're not headed into the president or CEO slots. That's just not what happens. So ascension plans have to reflect common business practices. They have to be logical and reasonable.

The thing that separates a plan from a wish list is that the planner has to *do things* to get to the goal. She doesn't just have a desire; she takes responsibility for creating the reality of that desire. Wishing, praying, chanting, and magical thinking may sell a lot of pop psychology books, but it is *doing* things that helps create a new reality. You have to take responsibility for actualizing your plan. No one else is in charge of making your ascension plan happen.

Your ascension plan needs to cover at least these topics and follow a logical, step-by-step path:

1. Select **specific job titles** that you would like to get next, with realistic career paths to reach those goals.

2. Create a logical plan to **obtain the skills** necessary to perform in the desired position(s), or more to the point, create a plan that represents your exposure to and capacity for those skills.

3. Create a realistic self-promotion plan to **sell yourself** as ready and available for such roles.

4. Create a feasible plan to **replace yourself** and exit gracefully from your current assignment.

5. And finally, prepare for all the **triggers and contingencies,** thought out ahead of time, that drive each part of the plan.

Fast-Track Careerists

My own work as a career coach has focused on working with highly ambitious people. I define a fast-track careerist as one who gets a promotion every year to eighteen months. These careerists are just more interesting to work with than regular people. They make their own breaks. They never sit around and talk about what they "shoulda, woulda, coulda" done if only someone would have given them a break.

They are not afraid to change jobs; they are not afraid of periods of unemployment; and they are not afraid to challenge their bosses when their bosses are wrong. They seek opportunities to learn new things and face new challenges. They are not afraid to change and evolve.

On the other hand, they are often not the most emotionally well-balanced people. They are eternally dissatisfied. They care far more about their careers than anything else, often to the detriment of their marriages, their kids, their communities, and so on. They sacrifice their personal lives to their work accomplishments. Perhaps they should all just go into therapy, but a lot of organizations would certainly be in trouble if they did!

There are two distinct kinds of people in the world: People to whom things happen, and people who create their own reality. *Fast-track careerists are always people who create their own reality.* Whether you decide to pursue the career patterns of a fast-track careerist or not, we all can learn a lot about getting promoted by looking at what they do.

Even if you abhor the career-first mentality, take the tips and techniques that you need in order to get the promotions and assignments that you want, to get you where you want to be, and to make you happy.

A Word of Caution

Marquesa D. had a plan to get promoted in her property development company in California. When it didn't happen on her time line, she quit her job and started to look for a more promising opportunity. But she made the fatal error of quitting in the face of an historic property correction. There was simply a contraction in her industry at a critical time for her, career wise. She ended up patching together some consulting assignments for a year before going into a government agency with lower pay and much more pedestrian career potential. So before you quit any job, take a cold look at the market. It is almost always better to look for employment while you are employed. You always have to match your career moves to greater economic and industry trends. Of course, you can beat trends if you are lucky. But that's not the way to plan. Salmon swim upstream, but then they die.

Being Honest about Skillsets

One of the hallmarks of emotional maturity is the ability to objectively assess and analyze yourself. It is important to be able to make a list of traits, strengths, and weaknesses that fairly accurately reflect what others would list as your traits, strengths, and weaknesses. It is invaluable for you to be able to see yourself objectively, the way others see you. Not everyone can do this.

In fact, there is some research that indicates that many incompetent people are completely and continuously self-deluded about their skills, abilities, and contributions. They actually *believe* they are doing a great job when they are woefully incompetent. They are usually a drag on everyone around them. If they were removed today, the organization would be better off tomorrow with no one in their place. Fortunately, they rarely rise very far in the ranks because they are not in charge of their own ascension. Unless nepotism is involved, their careers will consist of a series of laterals, moving on when they get fired or when it dawns on them that the people around them just don't appreciate their awesomeness. It's not surprising that similar research indicates that arrogant people do not realize that they are arrogant. They too are clueless.

So your job as a careerist is to prepare your skillset not so much to excel in your current assignment, but to get promoted to your next assignment. You have to *anticipate* the skills you need for possible promotions and seek to gain mastery or at least exposure to those functions. If you're going to be in charge of staffing in your next assignment—write a job description, or get assigned to a search team for a critical new hire. If you're going to be in a P&L role next—offer to provide part of the data collection and analysis that goes into financial reporting on your current business unit. If you're going to be selling to Europe—study German or French language tapes at night, take your next vacation there, and drop by to meet some key people.

By the way, because you will be seeking a promotion, you also want to analyze the skills *and deficiencies* of the executive you will be seeking to replace. When the H.R. function plans for succession scenarios, they assess the skillsets needed to perform in each role. They do not do this in a vacuum, but within the context of the organization that exists today. Thus, they will look coldly at the deficiencies of incumbents and plan a wish list of improvements they will seek in the next person to hold that key assignment.

In some ways, they are like the newly divorced. They may not have a clear idea what positive attributes they are looking for in their next spouse, but they are absolutely sure what negative attributes they want to avoid next time. They are looking for new partners *without* the big deficiencies of the last incumbent. Because of this, trivial weaknesses can end up more important in a placement decision than important, critical strengths. This is human nature, and you can use it to your advantage. For example, if the old VP was a hothead, *your* even temper can be even more attractive than your degrees or certificates. If the old VP was late with critical assignments, *your* timeliness might be seen as even more of an asset than your technical skills. If the old VP was a boob overseas, *your* success traveling abroad and dealing with foreign clients might outweigh other insufficiencies. Understanding this lets you more subtly allocate your resources. Instead of just preparing to excel in the new role, prepare to contrast yourself favorably with the person currently holding the job.

So, begin an accurate assessment of your own skillset and then the needed skillset. Then perform a classic gap analysis, and develop a plan to bridge that gap. Don't demand of yourself that you master every needed skill. Sometimes exposure is all you need, and sometimes a mitigation plan is sufficient. If you can explain how you will perform successfully without acquiring the needed skill (for example, hire an interpreter instead of learn Chinese or bring along a trusted financial officer instead of go back to school for two years), then you may get the nod.

Managing the Review Process

Everybody has worked somewhere where "annual" reviews run months late as procrastinating managers keep putting them off. The truth is that most managers dislike the annual review process. They hate the paperwork, they hate having to tell subordinates what they're doing wrong, and they abhor the arguments over who should get a raise and for how much. No wonder they try to avoid it. And employees may have similar trepidation about the review process because most people dislike criticism, because it's so hard not to take personally.

But smart careerists have a totally different attitude. They know long in advance when annual reviews are *supposed* to occur, and they prepare to manage the process in their favor.

First of all, they have a running brag sheet from which to pull review material. They prep their boss with material worthy of a quick copy and paste into review forms. ***By controlling the story, they control the outcome.*** Don't hesitate to prepare a sheet of talking points and hand them to your boss, saying something like this: "I know that annual reviews are coming up, and I thought I'd just give you a progress report on my activities for the last ten months."

Think of having categories like this on your memo to your boss:

- ☐ Wins that are presented to show you in the best light.

- ☐ Losses that are presented in a way to minimize your fault. Obviously you will want to minimize reports of losses, altogether.

- ☐ Areas where you feel you have excelled.

- ☐ Areas where you would like to improve your skillset in the coming year.

- ☐ Concrete plans to improve your skillset in the coming year.

- ☐ New challenges in which you would be interested, should the opportunity arise.

In other words, *you provide the entire content of your performance review to your employer so that she does not have to do it, and so that every interpretation favors you.*

It is important to note that you can deflect a focus on your shortcomings by presenting a plan to overcome them in the coming year. If you bring a concrete, executable plan to soften your rough edges, support or ameliorate your weaknesses, and further refine your performance, many a manager will not feel the need to focus on your failures.

Finally, get on your boss's calendar! If *you* set the date for the review, it is much more likely to be timely. Act like a dentist's office, and remind your boss of the upcoming appointment: "Don't forget we have my review on Monday, so I hope by then you'll have filled out H.R. form AR-12/L12-15 available at www.companyintranet/HR/AR/forms.html. Your intranet password, in case you haven't used it lately, is boss719. Thanks! And I look forward to talking about goals for next year on Monday at 9 a.m. in your office!"

Accelerated Reviews

One way to break out of the pack at any company is to get an accelerated review. When you are hired, or anytime you take on a new role, you can negotiate that your performance review will be accelerated to six months or nine months out, instead of the usual twelve. You can also benchmark your review, tying it to some clearly identifiable accomplishment, such as, "I'll get a review upon opening the new office in Sydney and generating our first $1 million in revenue there." Both compensation and title are appropriate to reconsider in a review like this.

An accelerated review is particularly apt if you cannot come to terms on your salary or your title. So, if you accept less salary than you ideally want, try to get an accelerated review. If you are meeting or exceeding your goals by that date, you should expect to be elevated to a pre-agreed salary level. Very often, you can negotiate the removal of the word "acting" from your title at a certain date or upon completing an important task.

One problem with accelerated reviews is they often don't happen! When organizations want you to take an assignment, they'll promise you almost anything. But then inertia sets in, and you'll be lucky if your annual review happens every fifteen months. The best advice: get this promise in detail and in writing, and file a copy in your personnel file and keep a copy yourself. Even then, many organizations will default to their norms.

Counterattacking a Bad Review

Software engineer Austin R. had two bosses, one in charge of his project management work and one in charge of his software development. The software development boss gave Austin a timely review, all positive, and praising his skills. The other boss waited until the review was six months late and then blasted him. Austin never saw this coming. It was a stinging review, exactly the kind that someone gets shortly before being fired.

This second boss excoriated his supervisory skills, pointing out that Austin had two "partially substantiated" H.R. complaints from subordinates. One was a written complaint about his autocratic style, for which Austin had gone to a hearing and had apologized and agreed to take some additional supervisory training. The second complaint accused Austin of racism and sabotaging the employee's career, when in fact the employee was guilty of software plagiarism. Austin thought this was totally unfounded and protested vigorously. In both hearings he felt he had prevailed on fundamental principles but lost on style. But two complaints in one year is one too many for almost anybody.

Austin felt that he was being set up to be fired, so, in a brilliant counterattack, he fired off a memo to his boss, protesting that if these charges were serious, he should have been informed immediately. The fact that they had left him in place for an entire year would indicate that they did *not* see his supervisory skills as dangerously insufficient as the review implied. Then, he went immediately to H.R. and worked out a "correction plan" for his shortcomings, thus neutralizing a potential enemy. He also met with his two complainants to work out any residual, unresolved feelings about this. Finally, he pointed out that supervision was only 15 percent of his total responsibilities according to his personnel file, and he extracted an offer from his other boss to add that much work load should he be relieved of his supervisory duties. He did all this within forty-eight hours of receiving the review, and it no doubt saved his career.

Dealing with a Rival: Interview with Rob M.

"I was running this technology company that I owned a piece of, so I was in pretty good shape. I was pretty happy. I was the CTO, but the principal investor just let me run the company. He didn't even have an office in our building. We had a few million in revenue, a few dozen employees, a typical service bureau-type shop. I was good at solving problems and—no bragging—I was the best tech guy in the shop, bar none.

"Then I got a rival in the office, and I didn't really catch on right away. So we recruited this sales guy, VP of marketing, who was supposed to bring in new business. While I'm putting out fires and driving the techies, he's supposed to be out glad handing. What I didn't know was that this guy was sticking a knife in my back on a daily basis. He told our principal investor that I was a lousy leader, that I spent all my time doing stuff over that had already been botched by my guys, when in fact he didn't have a clue what I was doing. I did spend a lot of time in the field, but it was because I was the go-to guy when they ran into problems. In the meantime, the new guy wasn't producing. He was working up bids without any engineering input. He didn't know what he was doing. It was a mess. And there was very little new business.

"So the principal investor gets a little impatient and hires this outside consultant to evaluate our operation. He comes in and charges us a fortune to tell us what I already knew, that in the two years we had this sales guy, almost *no* new sales could be traced to him. But then the sales guy played a card no one expected. He says he wants to buy out the company. So the consultant, the principal investor, and this guy all have a love fest, and it turns out that he doesn't have any money. Meanwhile, I'm just doing my job. But when the dust settled, the principal investor names the consultant CTO, they keep the sales guy, and my shares are valued at pennies on the dollar by the same consultant who replaced me!

"I'm fired, I got robbed on my equity, and I never saw it coming. My advice? Never ignore somebody sticking a knife in your back. I should have spent more time on my relationship with the principal investor. I thought it was enough just to do a good job, but it turns out I was wrong."

Replaced by Three People: Interview with Mateo G.

"After a staff member left, and another guy got fired, I was covering the work of three people. I worked hard but I guess I made it look too easy. I put in for a raise, and in spite of my extra workload and heroic performance, I was told they only give raises once a year. So after seven months, when they refused to give me a raise, I just walked out the door with one week's notice. To hell with them. Their failure to be flexible cost them at least $50,000, and probably more, to hire and train three people to replace me. Then they had to pay three salaries instead of one."

Asking for a Raise or a Title Change

How do you ask for a raise or a title change? You have to build a business case for these types of requests and show that the raise is warranted not just because of your performance where you are now, but because of industry norms and the current career marketplace.

Before you start an action like this, you need to consider that asking for a raise or a title elevation is dangerous. Some bosses who were perfectly happy being your champion, who thought they were doing a good job of shepherding your career, will find it offensive and aggressive if you ask for a raise or a title elevation out of sequence. So negotiating these issues aggressively *when you are promoted or reassigned* is much less risky than making a play while you continue to hold the same assignment. Tying these moves to reassignments makes them much less contentious, so you need to provide specific accomplishments *that were above and beyond expectations* that warrant your salary (or title) advancing above and beyond expectations. Note that this is very nearly the exact same memo that you use to manage the review process. If you have no extraordinary wins to put in a memo, you will have very little to base your appeal on.

You can also bring in the issue of the career marketplace. Has the company begun to fall behind the curve on salaries? If so, they may not even realize it. Showing them recruiting notices for jobs exactly like yours but with higher pay or a fancier title, can sometimes be a deciding factor. No company *really* wants to fall behind the curve, because they know that the consequences are a flight of talent—while the deadwood is sure to remain.

Appeals for specific titles can be based upon industry norms, intra-organizational norms, or more subtly, on the need to impress clients. If your stakeholders are VPs at other companies, you can claim a need for a VP title. If your clients are high-net-worth families, you can point out that they would be more comfortable interacting with a managing director than with an account executive, and so on.

Again, the best time to negotiate title and compensation adjustments is when your assignment changes, or just after you have posted an extraordinary win.

The Final Word on Ascension Planning

Although I have been talking mostly about promotions in this book, I really am trying to address the career-planning needs of highly ambitious careerists. There are many advantages to extracting every possible promotion from an organization before you decide to turn away from that organization and seek opportunity elsewhere. But you have to carefully weigh many factors, such as your marketability, the condition of the labor market in your industry at any given time, and the possibility of opportunity later with your current employer versus the risk of switching employers now. Sadly, few employers feel any loyalty to their employees today, which means your loyalty may not be rewarded, in spite of any assurances your boss may have made to you.

Which brings me to my final word on ascension planning. Any ascension plan *must* include triggers to leave the organization. It is very rare for someone to work for the same firm for thirty years anymore. Almost everybody will have to change jobs, and sometimes industries, to keep advancing over a long career. Anyone can get through a two-year dry spell, but anytime you're looking at more than two years without change, without increased responsibility and new tasks and projects, if you're stagnating, you need an escape route. You need to leave.

One very common trigger for fast-track careerists is an *emergency escape clause*. They do *not* stay in unpromising situations. They do *not* stay stuck. If they don't get promoted within a set amount of time, they will create their own opportunity even if it means making a lateral move or changing jobs and employers.

It should be noted, however, that it accelerates your career to wring every promotion out of an employer before switching employers. And it looks much better on your resume! No matter how many promotions (or lateral moves) you take within the same company, no one will accuse you of being a job hopper. But if you change employers too often in order to achieve your advancement, you may not look attractive when you find yourself absolutely needing to change employers. In a rising tide, this is not that big a problem, but in a downturn it can be quite a liability.

Just remember, *it is always better to look for a job while you have a job.* Headhunters always prefer to advance employed candidates, as those candidates are presumed to be "off the market." Accessing "off the market" candidates is the root justification for involving a search professional in the first place. Employers assume that employed people are more valuable than unemployed people, and indeed, unemployment itself is risky. If it goes on too long you can have shelf-life issues.

So learn to change jobs, to conduct job searches while still employed, and to place yourself on the market smoothly and with aplomb. Switching employers to get out of a dead-end career path is a critical long-term career-management skill.

Do You Really Want a Promotion or Do You Just Want to Change the Rules?

If you want to change the rules where you work, there's an old saying that comes into play: *If you want to change the rules of the game, you have to win the game first.*

If you prove yourself first by showing your employer the huge return on investment that employing you provides, then he will be more likely to entertain special requests from you about your working conditions.

Tyler B. was tired of getting to work at 9 a.m. for her job as an accounting clerk in the Loop in Chicago. She hated the early crowds on morning trains, when there was plenty of room starting at 9:01.

Since she worked exclusively for one tax partner, she went to her and stated her case: She was hourly; always delivered in a pinch; was completely productive without supervision, so if she worked alone late in the evenings, the work was always good. She even threw in a little ego massage for her boss: "You're one of the senior partners here, and I'm pretty sure you can do whatever you want." Tyler got permission to come in "anytime before 10" as long as her billable hours stayed the same, proving that exceptional employees can effect exceptions to the rules and bring about a positive policy change. Based in part on the success of Tyler's unique work rules, her firm eventually adopted a core hours model, and *everyone's* commute was eased!

Coleman W. was a master carpenter who did displays and cabinetry for an old-line department store in San Francisco. He was supposed to work six to two, Monday through Friday. But Coleman didn't like to work five days a week because it interfered with his leisure pursuits, which mainly consisted of surfing and hanging out with his friends. Coleman was a very good carpenter and always got the store open on time. Here's how he solved the problem: "I called in sick every Friday for six months, and eventually they just quit putting me on the schedule for five days. I really didn't care if they fired me, but in the end, everybody's happy." Not very mature, perhaps, but it got the job done.

One of my employees, Kathleen D., wanted to go back to school while she worked for me. She was, bar none, the most profitable and most productive employee I'd ever had. You better believe I accommodated her school schedule!

Companies are experimenting with customizing their work arrangements as they deal with several pressures on staffing: (a) strong competition for the most skilled employees and fear of a looming bidding war, (b) the well-established need to retain at least some of the services of employees who become parents, (c) changing demographics of young people at least temporarily favoring employees over employers, and (d) a retiring Boomer generation that is going to fade away slowly rather than just separate from employment on a specific birthday.

Far too many employees walk away from a job, and abandon the employer-employee relationship, without giving the employer a chance to fix what's awry. Here's my absolute rule for negotiating: *Ask for what would make you delighted.* Don't project your negotiating opponent's position; don't assume she won't be willing to give you what you want. So before walking away from any deal, ask for what would make you delighted. You'd be surprised how often you can get all or most of it.

If you want to work from home one day a week, quit traveling, be home before dark on Fridays for religious reasons, come in late, or skip work the first day back from a business trip, state your business case and ask for it. But be smart. Be valuable! If you're valuable, you have leverage. And know your boss: Some brain-dead bureaucrats wouldn't entertain a proposal like this even for a moment. If you work for a smaller company, or a smaller work unit inside a larger company, there may be more flexibility. But if you are one of twenty people with the same assignment, you're unlikely to get a break. It is vital to identify the decision-maker and state your case. The decision-maker may *not* be your boss (but your boss almost always has to back the change too). Offer a pilot test, so if it doesn't work out, you'll go back to the old rules. To make this a win-win negotiation, offer incentives: "I'll be more productive," "I'll be able to concentrate more," "Actually, I'll miss a lot less work," "It's certainly cheaper than hiring someone as a replacement for me," and so on. Be nice, not confrontational. Remember, it's a negotiation, not an ultimatum. If you absolutely have to, *and only if you absolutely have to*, give up a little cash if that's what it takes to get what you want. Giving up even a token amount allows them to save face and rationalize the change.

But do remember that if your employer has been looking for a chance to get rid of you, a push like this could be just the catalyst they've been needing.

What a Career Coach Can Do for You

Career coaching is not counseling, it's not therapy, and it's not being someone's friend. Career coaching is helping someone discover *their own solutions* to a career bind. Coaching, properly, is not telling someone what to do, but getting them to discover and develop a solution that comes from them and that they can, therefore, fully own.

I've been a career coach since before they even had a name for it. Over the years I have worked with almost every type of employee facing every type of challenge, but I did always focus on ambitious and talented people. Now I only coach executives, and I only coach through career transitions, such as taking on a new role or changing employers or navigating a crisis. Once the careerist masters the transition, I don't follow them in that new position. I like highly motivated people, powerful people, and I never wanted to get clients hooked on me like some of the coaches. I'm not saying there's not value in that, but it's not what I'm trying to do. I hand them off to others, who excel in providing ongoing counsel. I am about navigating rough spots, not incremental improvements once they are in place.

Coaching is not remedial. Coaching is about optimization. Highly talented people have coaches. Tiger Woods usually has more than one at any given moment, plus a caddy making suggestions on every hole. Olympic champions have coaches who could never beat them at the sports they are playing.

It is absolutely not true that everybody has to have a coach, and coaches who claim that are being, I think, disingenuous and self-serving. But an executive with a wise and confidential sounding board may find himself better able to avoid mistakes and better able to create innovative solutions.

Ironically, the higher one rises in the ranks, the harder it is to get objective and honest advice. CEOs are like rock stars and presidents, living in a bubble of information filtered by groupies. So coaching can be one source of honest feedback. The right kind of executive spouse is another, by the way.

Here is a case study from my practice.

EVP of Global Staffing

One of my favorite clients of all time came to see me over several years without ever changing companies. She was an H.R. officer in a large commercial bank. She still is. She had a meteoric rise from H.R. generalist as a young professional fresh out of college, to executive vice president in charge of global staffing. I followed her career all the way. She was the youngest VP in human resources they'd ever had, and now she has the top job.

Commercial banking is not filled with heavy risk takers, but her bank was entering a phase of truly dynamic change with a lot of mergers and new overseas exposure. Most of the senior managers were suffering from extreme stress. My client was hired at the start of this period, so she never knew any different. She was young, willing to work hard, and she wanted to advance quickly. While some of the older people around her were griping about all the changes, she was busy sussing out subtle shifts in the bank's strategy, and she had a knack for putting herself in front of the expansion.

There were three main keys to her success:

1. **She was honest.** I don't mean honest in that in-your-face, damn-the-consequences way, but if an idea stank, she could say so, *gently*, even if the idea came from upstairs. Someone else might have been burned at the stake for speaking the truth, but she always pulled it off.

2. **She was always ready with her documentation.** This might seem like a small detail, but I never had a client with better documentation. Her internal resume was updated at all times, and she was a fantastic business writer. She never had to tell someone, "I'll get back to you." She could always say, "I'll send it to you right now." Like all big organizations, new assignments were based on that internal resume.

3. Probably most important, **she was really comfortable with herself and confident.** You might think this was an inherent personality trait but not in her case. This woman's confidence and her ability to speak the truth came from the same thing: *She was always on the market.*

This is the area I was most involved with her. She ran a low-level job search outside her firm, more or less constantly. She interviewed for positions, she talked to headhunters, she had a disguised resume on most of the main boards, she took a lot of lunches with pals from other banks, she went to conventions—she did it all. This empowered her with the knowledge that she could change jobs anytime she wanted, which allowed her to be confident and speak the truth, which allowed her to stand out in this risk-averse crowd of bankers. Do you see how it worked?

She did the same thing inside. She spent a lot of time eating lunch with people with no project or reporting relationship with her. She had a much broader view of the bank than most people, especially when she was just getting started. She could see the bank as a whole, beyond her own assignments and her own department.

Every time it looked like someone might win her away from the bank, she got a promotion or at least some awesome new assignment. So she stayed. Eventually, she quit looking. But for a long time, being on the market was the secret to her career success.

The beauty is that the bank never really knew how many times she had offers to leave. She was *very* discreet about it. She pushed and pushed. It just happened that they won the negotiations every time—without even knowing they were negotiating to keep her.

Adjusting Priorities and Focus: Eboné J.

"I had been associate dean at a small liberal arts college, and I was moving to become associate dean at a Pac-10 school, but that is where the similarities ended. The new job would pay twice as much, and I would have seven assistant deans reporting to me. It was really a big move.

"The best advice I got was from an old hand who'd had just about every [appointment] at the university at one time or another. We went to lunch, and he told me who everybody was and about the personalities of all the key players. But the most important thing he told me was this: I would have to stop worrying about every single student because I would be unable to do my work—the job I was hired to do—if I let individual student's concerns eat into my day. I got into this line of work because I love college students and I love to serve them. I believe in the model of the servant leader. I mean, I'm dedicated. But his advice was right on the money.

"My job now is to set policy and provide leadership. I get work done through policy, and through having good people work for me. You have to know when to listen to a student who is telling you something about your policy. But if I still had my door open like I used to, I would be ineffective, and I would have failed at my new assignment.

"Here's how he worded it: What got me here will not now move me forward."

INTERVIEW WITH A
FAST-TRACKER, JASON L.

Well, let me tell you a little about me, and then I'll tell you how I got here and what advice I have for ambitious people. I've been promoted ten times in the last eleven years. I began as a research engineer and made it all the way to my current assignment as SVP of a *Fortune* 500 company. I'm not done yet. You can bet on that.

I have a law degree. I never did use it, although it's certainly a good credential. It impresses people. There are a lot of nonpracticing lawyers out there, in the executive ranks. I just got the law degree for fun at night. You never know.

It seems that a lot of different things went into the different promotions. My first one was created for me because they recognized my value and didn't want to lose me. I've done that same thing myself, as a manager. You see someone who stands out, and you give them a bigger challenge.

Twice I was promoted because I had a close peer who was not performing well. In both cases, I worked closely with those guys who weren't doing a solid job, and that accelerated the decision to eliminate the guy in that role. I was not trying to undermine them. Just the opposite, I tried to help them. In fact, both times they stayed with the company. But I got their people and their roles.

I did get promoted one time just the way that you commonly think of it. The incumbent left, and there were three people, and of the three, I was the best qualified and most experienced, so I got the assignment.

Once I got promoted out of spite. That's really the only way to describe it. I had problems with my previous boss, and the guy who came in to replace him promoted me because he didn't think much of the previous guy either. He moved me out of program management into quality, and although I've been very successful here, I wasn't really qualified for it. It was pure politics. The guy who is now CTO of the parent company and CEO of our business unit had a long battle with our former COO of the parent company, who was also former president of our business unit. Right when my former boss got the approval to axe me, he was fired himself, and the new guy took control over our business unit. He promoted me out of spite for the prior guy. It was nice for me, but I was really a pawn in a power exchange between these two much more powerful executives.

So how do you get noticed? Customers genuinely like me, and I have very good interaction with our own sales people. Being tied to revenue is always smart. Whenever I have access to people higher up the food chain from me, I make sure I take advantage of it.

You have to ask yourself who you are trying to impress and what impresses them. This is situational. It may be something different for every person, and even something different with the same person at different times. I customize based on what our current business strategy is. Even with the same customer, one time it is technology, the next time it may be how we're going to keep costs in line. You have to make sure you know his hot button at any given time, and make sure you're doing it in an active way.

You want a hot tip? Do your job. Pay attention to your bosses. Don't get off course worrying about peers. As much as I like a fight, because I'm half Irish and half hillbilly, it's always counterproductive. I've done it a couple of times, and it is nothing but a distraction. Take care of your bosses and they'll take care of you.

You want to know how to break out of the pack? Take a tough assignment. I've rewarded people for taking one for the team. Every company has projects that nobody likes, but somebody has to do them. If it's important to the company, and you do them well, with a good attitude and without bitching, and you make my job easier, then I'll reward that. An assignment only lasts six months to a couple of years. It's not like it's forever. That can create a break-out opportunity. A lot of people fear getting pigeonholed. That's almost never the problem. You do your job and make sure people know you're succeeding.

Ambition can become a problem if people are clamoring for notice all the time. Some execs see through that, and some don't. It depends on how good the person is at hiding it selectively.

Oh, yeah. I got one like that right now. I got a young engineer who just wants to go from engineer to senior engineer. He seems very concerned with what exactly he needs to do, but he doesn't have much experience doing much of anything. And he keeps getting in my face. We offered him a position in a new plant in Indiana, which he rejected. And then we offered him a spot in an existing plant in Kentucky, and he rejected that idea, too. He didn't even want to move. You're not going to have any luck waiting for a dream job. You gotta take what comes up. We brought him exactly what he had been asking for, and he trashed it.

He's not even on my radar for a promotion now. He's not on my list. I'm not going to bend over for this guy.

Another thing that is always counterproductive is to complain about someone I already promoted. It's obnoxious to claim that you do more work than that person. It calls my judgment into account. You're claiming I must be wrong about what I see in the person, and you think your sheer brilliance is going to convince me with your arguments that I made a mistake. Well, that doesn't go over very well, I assure you. And it happens more than you'd think. I hate whiners.

This is kindergarten rules, really. Do a good job, play nice with other people, do more than is expected, and be sure you're communicating well with the teacher.

And here's a thought: You have to be in a company with promotion opportunities. You can't squeeze blood out of a turnip. We've gone from being a $1.4 billion company to a $3 billion company, doubled in size, and they've had plenty of opportunity to reward talent with advancement. In real terms we've been growing right around 9 percent per year, and that's pretty healthy. If you're bumping along at 3 percent growth or suffering through a contraction or a downturn, you're not going to have this experience no matter how talented you are.

CHAPTER SIX

ALWAYS MAKE YOUR BOSS LOOK GOOD

You Are Closely Tied to Your Boss

Your boss has enormous power over you, and direct impact on your success. She can credit you for successes and blame you for failures whether such credit or blame is warranted or not. She has control over your reputation both informally and formally. She can gossip about you or praise you to others. If she says good things about you, that is your reputation. Or if she chooses, she can tell stories about you that create another kind of image, such as that you are bumbling, incompetent, arrogant, sexist, slutty, dangerous and unpredictable, or not the brightest bulb in the pack.

She administers your official performance reviews; as a commentator said early in the book, she can be the author of your history and thus she can impact your career long after she is no longer your boss, and even after she leaves the organization.

She can give you meaningful assignments and help develop your skills, or she can constrain your ability to have any impact on the organization. If you create great ideas, she can forward your ideas around the company with your name still attached to them—or she can rob you and take credit for all your contributions.

Most people are painfully aware of this power of position held by any boss. But this is only part of the equation. What about the *indirect* impact of your boss on your career?

No matter how well you do your own job, your reputation and future are closely tied to your boss's reputation and future. Your power, prestige, and opportunity flow through her. If your boss is wounded, you are wounded. If your boss looks good, you look good. ***If your boss is promoted, you are far more likely to be promoted.*** And if your boss gets fired, you are *far* more likely to get fired, either at the same time or by the person who replaces your boss.

Like it or not, it is in your self-interest to pay close attention to how your boss is doing, to her reputation and standing with key personnel further up the food chain. These indirect forces can be just as powerful as any direct impact your boss has on your career.

How You Can Help Your Boss

Obviously, one of the best ways to make your boss look good is to do a great job. If you bring in your deliverables on time and in excess of expectations, you are clearly a contributor to your boss's success, and you are helping make your boss's area of responsibility a contributor to the enterprise.

What else can you do? Here are a few suggestions:

- ☐ Learn when to share and when to grab credit.

- ☐ Don't gossip about your boss. *Just don't do it!*

- ☐ Give the boss the information that matters.

- ☐ Do not be the source of surprises.

- ☐ Bring solutions when you bring problems.

Subordinates also have power over the reputation of their superiors. So use that power to make your boss look good. This is not an act of altruism. Remember, your reputation is directly linked to hers. If you tell other people about the good things that your boss does, then you are indirectly praising your business unit, of which you are a part. The unit wins are your wins.

There are bad bosses out there, certainly. But most bosses are sometimes good at being managers and supervisors and leaders and sometimes not very good at being the boss. The point is, you want to be a glass-half-full communicator. Talk about the good stuff, keep the bad stuff either to yourself or between you and the boss privately.

Think of your department as a family. You might fight bitterly within your family, but to the world, you present a united front. It works the same way in an organization. If someone outside criticizes anyone in your immediate family, you would rise to defend them. Likewise you should defend and promote your boss, even if you have "issues" with her.

How Not to Answer the Phone: Interview with Luke M.

"This all got started when our VP and group leader came back from some seminar about super service or the wow factor or something like that—some fad that was going around at the time like a bad cold. So he decreed that every department was going to have to start answering our phones with live humans. This goes against every idea of efficiency that I understand, but what can I do? I'm just one guy.

"The first thing they did was program the phones to ring on every desk in the department until someone answered it. This was unbelievably stupid and disruptive, and you couldn't turn it off. So my team leader decided we would hire somebody to answer the phones. This was so last century.

"So we hired this young woman who was a little informal during the interview process. I actually voted against her, but I was overruled by our boss. She was supposed to be our sales assistant, but of course she didn't know anything about sales. In fact, she didn't seem to know anything about anything. And she dressed like a tag sale. But I'm stuck with her.

"Then one day I come back from down the hall, and I actually hear her saying into the phone, 'He's down the hall in the bathroom. Do you want to hang on? I think he'll be right back.'

"Can you imagine that? My client has a mental image of me in the restroom. She's holding, thinking of what I'm holding. It's a miracle our girl wonder didn't say, 'He's in his other office.' What an idiot!

"Luckily, they got the word upstairs that this wasn't helping productivity; they turned the automated phone system back on, and we got rid of her."

Moral to the story: Everyone is always in a meeting, or on another phone call, or out of town for a conference. No one is late to work, no one is missing, and certainly no one is down the hall in the restroom.

Learn When to Share or Grab Credit

Who gets credit for a win is a touchy issue. In a truly fair world, credit would be shared according to the contribution to the win. But we don't live in anything close to a truly fair world.

Should you always share credit? When you are the team leader or function head this is a no brainer; crediting your team for their performance reflects immediately and directly back on you. It gets more complicated when you are that team player who is committed to the team, dedicated not to your own work but to the team's work. Being a successful team member is absolutely valued by modern organizations, but you also need to differentiate yourself. Because teams rarely get promoted as a team, you need to get the word out about *your* contributions to the team's success. So, in short, if you're a team leader, throw credit around liberally. If you're a team member, try to get some individual credit, if you can do it without being too obvious about it.

Finally, on this topic, if you have a boss who constantly steals your ideas and represents them as her own, you need to create a channel to inform people that the content originated with you, *and* you also need a new boss. Psychologists have found that at least 4 percent of top corporate executives are, in fact, sociopaths. They have no understanding, regard, or care for the feelings of others. Sometimes, the smart move is to move on.

Don't Gossip About Your Boss. <u>Just Don't Do It</u>

Perception is reality, and you want the perception of your business unit to be one of cohesion, productivity, intelligence, and contribution. Mud that gets on your boss gets on you. Thus, you certainly don't want to be the source of any mud thrown at your boss.

Gossip is dangerous in general, and gossip about your boss is radioactive. If it gets back to your boss, he will use his power of position to neutralize you. Disloyalty will be punished much faster and much more vigorously than incompetence. An incompetent sycophant has plenty of job security when compared to a competent malcontent.

If you have real complaints about your boss, keep them to yourself or exercise them in appropriate channels, such as face-to-face with the boss, or in private with an H.R. officer.

Remember, the knife you stick in somebody's back has your fingerprints all over the handle.

Give Your Boss the Information That Matters

To help your boss look good, help him do his job better by giving him the information he needs for timely and prudent decision-making.

In a knowledge economy, you serve as a filter for information to your boss. Are you a good and effective filter, or do you let toxic waste get through or even worse, occasionally let it stop up the pipeline entirely? Do you provide too much information, needlessly distracting your boss with minutiae? Do you withhold information critical to your boss's role, leaving him unprepared for risks you see looming on the horizon?

A helpful subordinate filters information appropriately. Doing this effectively makes you a desirable and respected associate. Do it poorly makes you a nightmare to supervise.

Knowing what information your boss needs is an inexact science. One boss may want to know once a year whether or not you are going to meet your annual objectives, while another boss will want progress reports by the hour. One approach is not better or worse than the other; they are just different styles. Your job is to discover and adapt to your boss's style.

I had the misfortune to have two office managers in a row who were equally poor filters. They were exact opposites of one another. One filtered almost nothing, and the other filtered everything.

At the time, I was running a rapidly growing career-counseling firm. Since I was traveling a lot, in my absence my office manager was supposed to be my eyes and ears in the office. I inherited an office manager who saved up every problem and dumped them on me as soon as I got off the plane. If I was gone too long, she called me with lists of issues. There was no problem too trivial for her to take to the boss. If we were out of paperclips, she wanted to know what size box to buy. If one person said something mean to another person, I had to hear all about it even if the problem had already blown over. I could have done her job itself in about the same amount of time it took for me to help her do her job.

A lot of young people spend *way* too much time running everything by their boss. They are hesitant to make decisions on their own and need constant feedback. This is actually reflected in their language. Instead of owning a problem or mistake or guaranteeing performance, they say "I'll try" or "I'll do my best," when what the boss wants to hear is "I'll take care of it," "I'll handle it. You can count on me," or "Don't think about it for another moment. I've got it under control."

I replaced the first office manager with a woman who assured me that she did not need micromanaging. What I did not realize at the time was that I may have complained a bit too much about the habits of the first office administrator. Subsequently I got *no* information about what was going on in the office. Whenever I called in and asked how things were going, she always answered, "Great. Everything's going just fine."

But sometimes things were *not* fine, and I had no vision with which to steer the office. I found out that a young career counselor I had hired into his first professional position was treating the support staff in a very mean and negative way. Plus there were accusations of racism, to complicate the matter. Instead of being able to address this problem when it first arose, I was blindsided when some of my best and longest-serving support staff threatened to quit. What could have been solved with a sit-down talk near the beginning of the troubles had festered into a need for a full-scale organizational intervention.

And there were other unpleasant discoveries. In short, I could not manage the business without information because my primary information filter was completely stopped up.

When you are uncertain whether to carry news to your boss, admit it. Especially if you are dealing with a rumor or something tangential to her area of responsibility. It's okay to go in and say, "I'm not sure if this is important or not, but I just wanted to run this by you. Do you have a moment?" If it's not important, you'll find out fast enough. If it is, you'll be appreciated for bringing it to her attention.

It is your job to discover how much and what kind of information your boss needs and when she needs it. The better you do this, the more you will be appreciated, and the better your boss can be at doing her job. And the better she is at doing her job, the better you look as part of her team.

Do Not Be the Source of Surprises

What a boss expects of a direct report differs as you rise up in the organization. At the bottom, in the types of jobs one has in the first ten years of a career, the boss is looking for performance and for appropriate information flows. But near the executive suite, the boss starts to want something else—she wants not to have surprises.

A supervisor near the front lines might tell a subordinate, "Surprise me" or "I don't care how you do it, just get it done." But an executive reporting to a senior executive would *never* get that advice. In the executive suite, being a source of surprises is almost always a bad thing, even if the surprise is positive. For example, suppose you have more revenue than expected, the response at the top is going to be: You should have had more accurate projections.

Think of the function head or chief executive as the pilot of an airplane, but this pilot sits in a windowless cockpit, surrounded by people providing data flows. The top executive flies the airplane based on the data that she is given by subordinates. When that data is off *either way* it is much harder for her to fly the plane effectively and safely, to the chosen destination, using the least amount of fuel.

Being a source of bad data, that is, being a source of surprises, is to put the entire flight at risk. So being the source of surprises is a career killer in the executive suite. Having a nonstellar but predictable track record can, in fact, be much better than having a reputation for occasional but unpredictable brilliance.

Bring Solutions When You Bring Problems

One thing we all hate to do is to be the bearer of bad news. If you avoid this necessary evil, however, you are robbing your boss of timely access to critical information. Bad news is often more important than good news, because bad news usually requires a response. Delays in taking corrective action may exacerbate the problem that created the bad news in the first place.

So how do you deliver bad news? Here are two tips: First, use language and a tone that projects that you are about to deliver bad news, to allow the listener to emotionally prepare for the unwelcome information. This is quintessentially what speakers are doing when they say, "Are you sitting down?" or even, "I have some bad news and some good news. Which do you want to hear first?" So project that you are about to deliver bad news, and your listener will be better able to deal with what you are about to say. Try lines like this: "Unfortunately, I have some bad news about _____. Do you have a minute to discuss this?"

Use a flat, serious, somber tone. Joking about bad news may make *you* feel better, but it can backfire. Gloating over the misfortune of others can go horribly wrong in the emotional heat of the moment. If your worst enemy wrecked the company yacht during a tryst with the boss's spouse, your gleeful reporting of this event could cost you your job. They really do kill messengers.

If you can, offer analysis along with the facts. For example, offer an analysis of the ramifications of the event, not just the event itself. Better yet, provide a list of possible remedial actions along with the disaster report. If you have the authority to put a solution into play, it's best of all when you can report that you are "already on it."

Pollyannas

Pollyanna was the heroine of an early twentieth-century novel by Eleanor Porter. Pollyanna was the eternal optimist, whose glass was *always* half full!

Some people are pathologically optimistic, some are blind to the dangers around them, and others simply don't want to be the bearer of bad news. In any case, a Pollyanna is a dangerous team member. If you are on fire, don't you want someone to mention it? Do you want to ride in a car with someone who would not point out that you are about to crash? Do you want to follow a leader who never sees risk, someone who cannot realistically evaluate chances for success because for him they are always 100 percent?

As well as individuals, there are whole cultures in which subordinates must never point out any type of error or problem to their superiors, robbing the superiors of the wisdom and insights needed to make good decisions.

A boss who is a Pollyanna is like a gambler who thinks he cannot lose. It might be a great ride, but they always end up broke. You may as well go ahead and seek a promotion or transfer, because you won't like the way this trip is going to turn out.

Don't be a Pollyanna. Learn to communicate bad news in the right way so you can be a valuable team member.

How to Deliver Criticism

The first rule of delivering criticism is to criticize *only* to change future outcomes. Properly done, criticism is not about blame. Criticism is a form of instruction, to change future behavior. If the person you are going to criticize cannot change, there is no point in criticizing him at all. In that case, the adult thing to do is to just keep your frustrations to yourself.

Some people are hypersensitive to criticism, and what you believe to be a harmless remark can cut them deeply, thus harming morale. Criticism is a powerful tool to be handled with care. Just be sure you are interested in changing the person's behavior in the future to achieve a better outcome for him—as well as for everybody else. If that condition is not met, it might be best to forego criticizing anyone at all.

Forget about sarcasm and joking around—not a good way to criticize even the closest of compatriots. Use gentle language and plenty of qualifiers. "You might consider. . . ." "Just a little bit more next time. . . ." "If you get a chance. . . ."

Most of us have worked around people who think they are being helpful with critical comments, when really they are being aggressive and domineering. The structure of their language targets the person, rather than the behavior. They tend to say things like, "You know the problem with you is...," rather than, "When this comes up next time, it might work out better if you'd...." When criticizing, focus on behaviors and responses to events, and don't generalize into personalities. This is the business version of the maxim, "God hates the sin but loves the sinner."

Finally, use the **Sandwich Method**. Criticism is most palatable when it is sandwiched between praise, using this pattern: POSITIVE, sneak-in-a-negative, POSITIVE. If you are careful, with this technique you can criticize upstairs and sideways, as well as down the org chart. Here are some examples:

"You have a real talent for handling angry people. Next time a client yells at you, though, you might try just talking them down instead of giving a massive discount like this. With your interpersonal skills, I'm going to predict you can calm them down without it costing the company a cent. You might try that next time, just to see if you can."

"That was a great meeting you just ran. I did notice, though, that you asked the only woman in the room to collect everyone's lunch orders. You have to be careful about that. You sure wouldn't want to get a reputation for doing stuff like that. But you really seemed to have everyone's attention, and I think you had excellent answers during the Q&A."

"I was really honored that you picked me to go on the client site visit. It would probably have gone better if you'd have had a chance to look at those product specs though. I think I can cover for what you promised, so I don't think it's any problem. Boy, do you know how to work a room. You really had them going with that talk about an antigravity field!"

No matter how long you might dress someone down, and no matter how thoroughly you go into every mistake they made, always end on a positive, hopeful note.

Managing Up

Managing up means focusing your people skills on those above you, the real stakeholders in your job. If your bosses are happy with you, that is certainly one version of success. Managing up requires different skills than managing down or laterally. You do not have much power over those above you, which fundamentally changes the dynamic. Some bosses are difficult to manage. In fact, some are difficult, period.

For more on how to manage these crucial relationships, read Michael and Deborah Singer Dobson's *Managing Up: 59 Ways to Build a Career-Advancing Relationship with Your Boss.*

Going Over Your Boss's Head

Sometimes your boss stands between you and what you need to get done in the organization. The more talented you are, the more likely this will occur on a regular basis. Being able to reach beyond your boss is very much a fast-track career skill, and knowing when not to do it is a crucial career survival skill, because it is so dangerous to go over your boss that often it is better to abandon a goal than to try to get past his blockage of it.

It is generally considered an act of disloyalty to go over your boss's head to get something done, to appeal a decision, to apply for an internal opening, or to distance yourself from something your boss has done. In most companies, it would be the beginning of the end of the relationship you have with your boss.

Before you go over your boss's head, make sure you've explored avenues to success that do *not* involve jumping over his position. Then and only then should you attempt to go around your boss. If you need to go over his head, the general rule is: Ask for permission first. If you violate this rule, you may never regain his trust.

As in criticism, couch your query in soft language with lots of qualifiers. Don't make it seem like a big deal. Here's an example: "Well, I hear you when you say this is a bad product idea, but would you mind if I run it past engineering to at least see if it's possible? They'll probably say the same thing you do, but still, I'd like to check it out if you don't object."

Of course, if engineering likes the idea, give at least some of the credit to your boss to make him look good, as in, "Yeah, that's great! My boss said I should run this by you guys, and I'm sure glad he did. I'll tell him you like it." But what do you do if he says no? Then swallow your idea and wait.

If you apply for an internal opening, sometimes, but not always, you can let your boss know after the fact. You always want your boss to know that you are not a lifer in the department, anyway, but make it seem like no big deal.

"I just wanted to let you know that I dropped a resume on an internal opening in San Francisco. I'm so not qualified for it, but you never know. Besides, I had this career development class in B school, and they said to interview once in a while just so you don't get rusty. Nothing will come of it, probably, but I wanted to let you know in case someone calls you about it."

Remember, no surprises.

Access to Upstairs

Suppose you decide to violate the rule of not going over your boss's head without permission. Suppose your boss is a one-man forest of deadwood who sits on your creativity and/or steals your good ideas and sells them as his own. How do you get your message over his head?

First of all, be truly sure you are ready to leave the organization before doing this. You should never be afraid to leave an organization if you're not getting anywhere inside it.

Then, try one of these techniques:

☐ Wait until your boss goes on vacation or a long business trip.

☐ Go to a trade show, convention, or meeting without him.

☐ Start cc'ing decision-makers up and out on your emails and memos.

The most dangerous of these techniques is, perhaps, to start cc'ing decision-makers outside of your normal sphere of influence. For this reason, it is a good strategy to occasionally have contact with these people so that the first time you do so, it isn't to go over your boss's head.

The safest way to begin contacting these people, by the way, is to cc them on a brag or win report, where you give credit to your boss and your team for a job well done. Nobody, not even your deadwood boss, is going to complain about the address list for that type of email.

Another way to access two levels up from you is to simply wait until your boss is on vacation or out of town. Invent a need for a management decision, and voilà, you have a reason to jump a level on the org chart. While there, carefully bring up your topic. Believe it or not, I did this to sell a book to my publisher that had already been rejected by my editor. The publisher liked the book, and when the editor got back from vacation, it was already on the publication schedule! This is dangerous and not to be undertaken lightly. I had taken the trouble to change the title and explained to my editor that the book was "quite a bit different" from what he had rejected, but truth be told, it was exactly the same book. My editor forgave me. Maybe your boss will, too.

Be aware that some bosses will not leave town without safeguards in place. They will insulate senior management from you with either a complete list of contingency plans or by putting a lateral in charge of you for the duration or, worst of all, by giving explicit instructions for you to stay away from the next level of management during his absence.

Some deadwood bosses never take vacations at all. One way that corporate security officers search for embezzlers and thieves is to search company records for employees who never go on vacation. Embezzlers are famous for fearing investigation and exposure during an absence, so they are never absent. Some incompetent people use the same protective strategy.

The Schism

Suppose you try all of these techniques to get your message heard above the bell jar of your boss's fearful ego. Before you stretches a future under your deadwood boss that is bleak and devoid of potential. Your best next option is probably to leave the organization and look for more fertile soil.

This is the point of schism, when your interests and your boss's interests diverge: His interest remains to maintain a tight level of control on his sphere of influence, and yours changes from trying to make the best of it to just getting the heck out of there.

One warning: Creating a fight with your boss is usually just going to result in a bad reference. Exiting gracefully is always a good idea, and exiting gracefully from a bad situation is especially important. You never want to burn a bridge if you don't have to. One client I worked with through a resignation wrote a letter of appreciation in which he said, "And I want to thank _____ for teaching me I could work successfully with all types of people and succeed in all types of environments." The boss took it as a compliment!

You *must* sit through an exit interview and you *will* remember: *Business is great. People are wonderful.* If there wasn't room for advancement, and you decided to look for better prospects elsewhere, just skip the opportunity to lob a hand grenade into your business unit and depart with your dignity intact instead.

In the movie, *Jerry McGuire,* Tom Cruise's character writes an intra-office memo revealing all the hypocritical, self-serving practices in his office. He is fired within days. He then attempts to convince other staff to go with him, and all of his accounts are taken away. If you decide to throw a few shots at your soon-to-be-ex boss on your way out the door, the result is that you are almost sure to get injured in the process.

Only top executives should get involved in public fights with their colleagues, and only when the success of the enterprise is at stake. It is a moral obligation at that level to fight to the death for one's ideas, if you perceive the penalty for failure to be the demise of the organization itself. But this is the life of the gunslinger. It looks glamorous, but you can only lose once. The penalty for losing, in all too many cases, is that your career is over. For almost everyone, the best schism is a quiet separation. You can go on to fight your battles in another organization, where you have a higher chance of success.

Losing at Golf

I spoke with several fast-track executives who told me that their desire to make their boss look good extends all the way to the golf course. "I absolutely will not beat my boss at golf," said one, "even if I have to shank a couple into the trees. And you can always miss a putt if you have to. I'm at least as good as he is, but I only beat him once, and he seemed to be peeved about it. I never beat him again." If your boss ever found out you lost on purpose, the cost in terms of loss of trust might be great. So if you decide to adopt a boss-management strategy like this, be smart enough to keep it to yourself.

You might think twice before annihilating your boss in any sport, be it poker, "Jeopardy," darts, or picking up someone in a nightclub.

Does This Chapter Make You Uncomfortable?

Does it make you uncomfortable to think about working to make your boss look good? Do you resent the idea that part of your mission is to cover for your boss's mistakes? Is this type of activity already taking up way too much of your time and energy?

Then perhaps you have the wrong boss. You may need to get a boss you can support with minimal reservations. No one is perfect, but your boss and you have one of the closest bonds in business, and you share an interlocked future. If you cannot support him, maybe it's time to look for an internal transfer, and if that's not forthcoming, you may need to move on to a new organization.

Having an inspiring boss is motivational. If you are motivated, you will excel. If you excel, you will advance. It is a true career advantage to work around talented high performers. James Watson, co-discoverer of the structure of DNA, is famous for saying, "If you're the smartest person in the room, you're in trouble!" Being challenged by the best to do the best and be the best is probably going to launch you much further than standing out in a bunch of morons for the mere fact that you are not a moron.

Here's what one fast-track executive said to me about his own amazing career success, switching from a low-level position in a nonprofit to a series of promotions leading to a director-level position for a $2 billion company: "Try your level best to make sure you've found the right job, in the right area, within the right organization, and whom you feel good about it. Make sure you're working for a boss that you respect and admire, and who respects you and is concerned about your welfare and development. Your boss is critical. Those are the circumstances you need in place to have faith that your hard work and good ideas will be rewarded."

Is Your Boss an Introvert or an Extrovert?

Do you have to be an extrovert to make it to the top office? Absolutely not. Introverts are (on average) more creative than extroverts, and creativity seems to have much more career value than extroversion by itself. Although some studies I've come across say that people *believe* extroversion to be an advantage, the study that matters is from CPP, Inc., publishers of the ubiquitous Myers-Briggs test. They own fifty years of data from officially licensed tests, and they claim that introverts appear among the ranks of CEOs at about the same rate as they occur in the general population.

However, among women executives, extroversion seems to be much more of an issue. Women executives are about twice as likely to be extroverts as introverts, while men executives are only about half again as likely (pretty close to population norms). Even with these ratios, however, it remains true that one-third of women executives are introverts.

So how does an introvert survive in environments that favor the socially well lubricated? They fake it until they learn how to do it! They learn to *appear* extroverted! When it is important to do so, they can be as outgoing and expressive as any born extrovert. Many consider it just another skill to be learned, and over time they learn to turn it on at will. Interviews with introverted executives turns up comments like these, "No one knows I'm an introvert," or "People would probably be surprised to learn that I consider myself an introvert." They learn to act like extroverts when it matters, and then to retreat to the comfort of contemplative privacy in the hours of the day when it does not impede their effectiveness.

Either way—introverted or extroverted—you can learn to speak up and be effective on teams, whether that team is a board of directors or a batch of summer interns.

What's More Important?

"If you love what you do, it doesn't matter if you get promoted. If you don't love what you do, you're not very likely to do well enough at it to get promoted anyway. Bottom line, it's more important to love what you do than to get promoted. The key to *everything* is to find something you love to do and then get someone to pay you to do it."

—JEREMY W., O.D. CONSULTANT TO THE AUTO INDUSTRY

INTERVIEW WITH A
TALENTED LIEUTENANT, GEOFFREY J.

I was as an attorney with a law firm in St. Louis, doing very well, your basic junior associate, when I got a call from a friend of the family in [a Southern state]. He was going to run for sheriff, and he wanted me to help him win the election. I thought he was calling everybody he knew, but since he wanted me to run his campaign, that can't have been the case. He was very personal and very sincere.

This call was totally unexpected, and it created quite a dilemma for me. I grew up around this guy. He was a close friend of my father's. When I was a kid I used to play golf with them, and in college I'd been his office assistant for a couple of summers. He knew I could write a clever letter and manage administrative work flow. He knew I could think on my own and that I could be trusted. We'd always been active in politics, my family, backing candidates and helping with campaigns, but I'd never even thought about managing one.

Practicing law was a bit tedious. I could see the steps to partner, and just how that would play out for the next thirty years. It was hard work without being very interesting, but I had gone to a lot of trouble to get into a good law school and then get a job with a top firm. But then he said the magic words. "[Geoffrey], I want to be governor, and I think you can help me get there, step by step."

I was hooked. I have a thing about power. I'm drawn to it like a moth to flame. So I got a leave of absence from the firm, making up some story about how this guy could be a useful client to the firm some day. They almost never give leaves like that, but my request must have pushed some of the right buttons, because I got a leave to go manage his campaign. We ran a campaign like [that county] had never seen. No baby was unkissed, and no problem lacked a solution. Obviously we won.

So I became the director of administration for this county. In [this state], the county sheriff is really the top elected official. He runs law enforcement, as you'd expect, but he also runs the roads, the tax collection system, senior services, the healthcare safety net, everything. It's a big deal. Well this guy just turns to me and says, "You take care of all this. I'm going to start building the infrastructure for a run for governor." You know what the last thing he said to me was? "Don't make any mistakes. People are going to look at what we do here to see if I deserve to be governor. You've got two years, and then I'm going to run." That's all the direction I had.

So I ran this county for a couple of years. It was very exciting. I increased tax collections without increasing taxes, which allowed me to hire a layer of professional staff to oversee all the lifers we had to deal with in county administration. And I got my guy in front of the local news every week bragging about what a good job he was doing. The TV just loved him. He was a natural for media and I was behind the scenes, making it work. I just can't describe to you how much fun this was.

Then, the governor's campaign came along, and I discovered there was a whole new level. I taught myself how to use demographics, polling, voter data, zip code-level messaging, and all that. We hired the right consultants. My job was to spend his money to get the maximum votes, but his job was to go out there and get the money to spend. And he let me down. I am absolutely certain we could have won if he'd have delivered on the fundraising goals. We got beat by a better machine, and that's how politics works.

Now I am doing consulting on tax issues for a political consulting firm. I don't regret for a minute tying my career to this guy's dream. It was my dream, too. Those three years were the happiest of my life, really. We were doing something really big. And I did make a difference, a real difference. That county still has some of the best administration in the state. More services without more taxes. That's the best a government can offer.

CHAPTER SEVEN

SUCTION—
IT PAYS TO STAND NEXT TO
SUPERSTARS

The Physics of Suction

When any object moves through any medium, it creates suction behind it. When a superstar careerist moves rapidly up the ranks, anyone standing behind that person will experience a pulling upward. Every position that Person A vacates needs to be filled by someone, and it may as well be Person B, especially if Person B is a protégé of Person A.

In other words, it pays to stand in the shadow of extremely talented people. They create activity and movement, which in turn, creates opportunities for advancement. Advancement may come through outright promotion to fill in the position the talented person has just vacated, but it also may come from the mere commotion caused by the truly talented person. You may gain skills by taking on special projects spawned by the superstar, or, by being her close colleague, you might get to meet powerful and influential people that the superstar has attracted. A superstar can challenge you to go beyond your own comfort zone, inspiring you to excel and draw attention to yourself in your own right. When there is no excitement or activity, advancement pretty much comes from death and retirement, and assignments are based on seniority.

This benefactor isn't necessarily more talented than you; maybe they're just ahead of you, older than you, or more developed than you are at this stage in your career. Some careerists are reluctant to stand next to superstars for fear that they will be overshadowed by them and overlooked. *Unless you are incompetent*, there are myriad advantages to being associated with highly talented colleagues. In politics this is called coattails, and no politician would turn down a chance to be on the ticket with a political rock star who turns out the votes and creates buzz! It's what gets you elected. And it does not mean that some day you won't be the head of the ticket.

Of course, if you are incompetent, you don't want to be anywhere near a high performer. But if you are reading this book, you are probably not incompetent.

Leadership Development Programs

Some corporations have formal leadership development programs. Companies use them to identify high-potential employees and put them into formal programs to develop their skills and channel them to opportunities. Sometimes people are chosen for these programs due to a high GPA when hired right out of college, or they are nominated by their supervisors. The H.R. pros I interviewed for this book were of divided mind over the utility of these programs. Some thought that candidates in the programs often failed to sustain high performance, thus negating the main rationale for them; others thought that the factors producing high performance were so complex and little understood that there was no scientific basis for selecting some workers for participation; still others thought they produced resentment among the rank and file, which tends to be also a fertile source of high performers. No one should turn down a chance to participate in a leadership development program that provides training and increased exposure to promotion opportunities, but any worker can design and create her own leadership development effort, and that is the main premise of this book.

To Be Lieutenant or Not to Be Lieutenant

Some people align themselves with powerful people as their lieutenants, as supporters of the superstar, and others align themselves with the superstar as colleagues, team members, and back-bench talent. Lieutenants tend to follow the superstar all the way, their futures permanently intertwined. Colleagues, team members, and back-bench talent are only temporarily aligned with the superstar; it's more a marriage of convenience, over as soon as interests diverge.

Neither approach is wrong, but it is hard to switch from being a lieutenant to being a colleague. You have to be intentional in how you structure and represent this relationship.

I want to stress that there is no indignity or dishonor in being a lieutenant. There is a personality type that makes an outstanding lieutenant: Someone hypercompetent, well organized, good at execution, but who often does *not* want to stand up front and dodge the incoming rocks and arrows. They take pride in being part of a talented dyad and, frankly, most leaders *cannot* succeed without them. They are an important and necessary part of organizational efficacy. But a lieutenant would be unlikely to get the top spot, while back-bench talent is being groomed precisely for that ascension.

Getting Promoted as a Team

Over the years I have worked with many top officers who rode a series of moves created and driven by someone else. The superstar was moving like a shock wave through and between organizations, and the careerist's main job was to keep being worthy of the opportunities that were dropped in his lap.

For a young person strategizing for career advancement, the lesson is to try to maneuver yourself to be chosen to accompany a rising superstar. When she gets promoted, you get promoted.

Senior-level function heads almost always like to surround themselves with some loyal troops. A smart CEO, president, or CFO wants to surround herself with people she can trust, people she has known for years, people who owe her for past favors. A top officer who doesn't come with her own colleagues and spies is simply not politically savvy.

Anyone who gets promoted is an agent of change. They are causing change in the unit they leave, and they are authoring change in the unit they join. When you know someone who gets promoted, analyze both ends of this event to see if you can find a spot for you to get promoted or perhaps just increase your authority, budget, privileges, or head count.

Moving Up Together

Seven healthcare lawyers and a paralegal switched firms together, as a team, in Houston in 2006. This allowed some senior associates who had been denied partner status at the old firm to achieve it immediately in the new one, and it allowed a close-knit team to keep working together. The firm that recruited the team was well known to have a high associate satisfaction rate. One can only assume that the firm that lost the team regrets not advancing some of these lawyers to partner before this embarrassing public exodus.

Advantages

The most obvious advantage to riding suction is that it creates promotion opportunities. But there are other valuable advantages. Superstars often challenge others to strive for and achieve excellence. *You never want to be the smartest person in the room.* You want to work with people who understand you, who appreciate and encourage your ideas, and who can guide you and help you develop. Superstars tend to collect friends, information, and connections as they move through life. Having a superstar as a close colleague gives *you* access to those people and that information. Remember, fast-track careerists tend to prefer obtaining their information from people in real time, rather than from databases. So, having a superstar just an IM or phone call away means you have that immediate information too. And a superstar who has your back can introduce you to people who can be of tremendous benefit to you, in terms of getting jobs, solving problems, doing favors for others—who will then owe you favors—and so on.

Superstars have a magnetic field of power around them. They make great guardian angels and benefactors as the petty politickers that inhabit all levels of management are afraid of them. If you are known to be favored by a superstar, your detractors will think twice before trying to harm you intentionally. (They may still harm you in myriad blundering, unwitting ways, however.)

Interview with an Anonymous Fast-Tracker

"I really don't want my name attached to this, but I'll tell you what happened. I was an investment banker, and I loved being an investment banker, but when [the president of the United States] got elected, I started getting phone calls. I guess all the former Presidential Scholars got phone calls, but I got a *lot* of phone calls.

"I got appointed chief of staff to the deputy secretary of a department which I won't name. I had been in the job for about nine months, when I got promoted by [the president] to become the second youngest person ever to hold my appointment. Bottom line, when I came on board, before the secretary was named, I did a diagnosis of what was dysfunctional in the department, and I moved out to fix that. Under the prior administration, this department had been allowed to languish; it had been neglected for years and it badly needed rehabilitation and reform. I had no agenda beyond the excellence of the organization; that was my goal.

"While they were actively searching to fill the open slot, I just started implementing my plan. I guess my apparent competence for leading organization change, the fact that my plan seemed to be working out perfectly—and I was getting along well with everybody, and people seemed to want to follow me, follow my leadership—got noticed. They said, 'He's already doing that stuff anyway.' I got the job because I was doing the job.

"I ended up in a leadership role over all the other [people at my level], who were all a decade older than I was.

"My advice? You go out and assume you've got the role, and start behaving like you've got it. But it's important to note that I didn't do this in order to get appointed. I was just doing the job because that gap needed to be filled, and we couldn't wait, as a country, for Washington's bureaucratic gears to grind to a conclusion."

How to Identify High-Potential Colleagues

What does a superstar look like? When you see someone rising rapidly through the ranks, who keeps getting many, rapid, sequential promotions, he's either someone whose daddy's name is on the door or a potential superstar. When you see someone who is much younger than everyone she supervises *and* she is known to be hyper-competent, then she's a potential superstar. When you see someone who is an agent of change, who can change the direction of strategy or turn around business units from failure to success, then that may be a potential superstar. Superstars innovate and create at a pace noticeably higher than others around them.

You'll notice that I use the term "potential" superstar in the preceding paragraph. You only know someone is a superstar when they sustain this type of performance over a long period of time. Superstars can only truly be identified in hindsight. At first they may be lucky, or they may have entered the organization well below their skill level. But if they keep advancing on the org chart, evolving their skillset, and anticipating organizational needs over and over again, then they are likely to be the real deal.

Identifying highly talented people before they become famous in the organization is a useful career skill. Once a superstar becomes a known entity, she'll be mobbed by groupies and you'll have competition for her attention.

If you are an ambitious and highly motivated person, *actively look for high performers in the organization*. Attach yourself to their projects, and see if you can get them involved in your projects. Find ways to collaborate with them. Get associated with and involved in their success. Learn from them. Interview them and get their advice. Enlist them into your pantheon of guardian angels and benefactors.

At the very least, get high performers like this into your own inner circle of career advisors. You want to learn what they are doing and how they are doing it. Analyze their success, and let it inform your own career strategies.

And if you are already higher up on the ladder, don't be overly officious when it comes to superstars. They have ways of chewing up org charts, anyway, and realigning channels of power and information. Even if you are above them, give them special privileges above and beyond their station on the org chart, because favors you rain down today may be favors that rain down on you tomorrow.

The Downsides of Following Superstars and Why You Should Avoid Gunslingers Altogether

There can be downsides to being or getting involved with high performers:

- ☐ **Fatigue and stress.** Superstars spawn activity like a whirlwind, and there are certainly calmer areas to stand in any organization than next to a superstar. If you're going to choose to align yourself with a high performer, you can expect to work harder than everyone else.

- ☐ **Resentment.** Agents of change can generate resentment. If you are associated with a superstar, some of that resentment may be associated with you. This is often unavoidable, so be prepared for it.

- ☐ **Accumulated enemies.** Resentment leads to enemies, and some enemies have a long memory for pain. If you keep moving through the organization, leaving your enemies behind, this is not a problem; but if you get stuck at any point, you may be surrounded by people who are eager to exact payback.

In any organization, the force of the status quo is so powerful it's like the physical law of inertia. An object at rest tends to stay at rest. An object moving in a certain direction will continue in that direction and will not veer without an outside force acting upon it. An object moving at a certain speed will maintain that speed, neither speeding up nor slowing down on its own. *A lot of people in any organization are like objects in space, being controlled by the law of inertia.*

High performers are particularly skilled at forcing their will on objects that would naturally continue in stasis. Most people don't like change, and anyone who makes them change is going to be resented. That resentment can be dangerous, so it needs to be factored into one's career plans.

Some superstars are so charming and exude such leadership charisma that people follow them with a minimum of emotional friction. But even they will create a wake of impact and fallout from resistance to change. Obviously, if the superstar keeps moving, most of that impact will be *behind and below* her and not that much of a problem. But if she ever stops and has to endure a long assignment in place, then it becomes quite a different story.

One type of high performer is particularly dangerous to follow: the gunslingers. Gunslingers are brought in to create massive, immediate change. They put their reputations on the line *every single time.* They hold nothing back; every project is a do-or-die situation.

Being a gunslinger may seem glamorous. They have the total attention of the CEO and inordinate, if temporary, power. They instill awe and fear. But the problem with being a gunslinger as a career choice is that you can only fail once; then you're dead.

Gunslingers are definitely a type: He is the turnaround artist who chops and realigns like a drunken surgeon in a back-alley knife fight; the software release engineer who drives her team to exhaustion, meeting the deadline like a hero, but leaving a trail of burnout and blood behind her; the young executive with a short attention span, who creates an atmosphere of constant crisis and uses that sense of crisis to drive his projects forward. Gunslingers are to be avoided if at all possible.

By the way, a lot of CEOs are, in fact, gunslingers. A CEO who stumbles even a bit may not get another chance anywhere. It is easy for the company to get another CEO, but it may not be that easy for the CEO to get another top slot.

Knowing When to Get Off the Ride

It's very important to see when your interests and the interests of "your" superstar diverge. Andrew Fastow attached his career to Jeffrey Skilling at Enron and followed him all the way into the CFO slot while Mr. Skilling became CEO. Needless to say, he didn't get off the ride soon enough, and both were eventually indicted for their criminal activities there. When your goals no longer align with the path the superstar is on, it may be time to make your break.

A MAN WITH A LOT OF FRIENDS, TIMOTHY L.

I'm a lobbyist. My job is to know people, and because I know people, I've never had to look for a job, I've never applied for a job, and I've never been turned down for a job, so you could say I'm pretty good at managing my career. I'll let you be the judge of that. Today I'm [director of government relations for one of the largest corporations in the world].

I have two points for your book, I guess. The first has to do with having friends who can help you get jobs, and the second one I'll get to in a minute.

You *need* friends. When I was still in law school I worked summers for [the state attorney general], and he hired me part-time while I was finishing law school. When I graduated, I had my pick of divisions, and I chose criminal division. My two best pals worked there, and we could cover each other's cases. Michael was older, and every time he moved up, Johnnie moved up behind him, and I took Johnnie's spot.

The A.G. lost an election. So we're all out. I called a friend of my mother's, and got a job as a D.A. in [another city]. Michael got a job as a lobbyist for [a large energy company]. Then Michael goes to *another* energy company, and he calls me up to ask if I want to be a lobbyist? "I dunno," I said, "What's it like?" He said "It's the best job in the world." So on his recommendation, they put me in his spot.

One point I want to make right here: A friend can get you introduced to people, but after that, you have to deliver. You have to be worth your friend's trust. Michael knew I could do the job. He wasn't just setting me up as a favor to me.

So I am doing great at [this energy company], when it gets bought by Michael's energy company! But by then, Michael has moved on to the company I work for now. I'm with the smaller [energy] company, so I'm in trouble. We all knew we were going to be fired. We literally would come in to work and not have anything to do. And then we'd go to lunch and not come back.

This was the largest corporate merger in history at the time. And this made a lot of Oil Patch companies nervous, and they went to their local congressmen and said, "We need protection from these outsider raiders." They made a pitch for keeping the center of gravity for the energy business down there. They were getting some traction up on the Hill. They were fighting the merger.

[The bigger energy company] hired an outside lobbying team, and these crackerjack guys went in to [the Speaker of the House], with the two CEOs, and the Speaker's personal lawyer. The CEOs told the Speaker about how this was going to be good for America, a big long speech, and after they were done, the Speaker turned to them and said, "Yeah, that's all well and good, but what's going to happen to my old pal [Timothy L.]? Why isn't he here with you?" And so they have to promise that I'm in on the deal.

Now I don't know anything about this, see? And when I arrived in the morning, there were two guys packing up my desk and taking my pictures off the wall. They said, "Come with us." And by noon I was over at [the larger company], signing my new W-4. It was a lateral, but everyone else was fired, and I was the only one left standing from [the old company], out of forty people in the department. That's the power of friends. The Speaker of the House saved my job, because he knew me and he cared about what happened to me.

Obviously, I got the job I have now because Michael brought me in here, too. I'm leaving out a few moves, but you get the idea. Every time, I knew somebody, and they knew me, and they believed in me.

So what's my second point? You have to be there for your friends, deliver for them, too. Take care of people, along the way. Help everybody and it pays off. In fact, there's a currency in sharing the credit. First of all, the person you give the credit to appreciates it. Acknowledge their good deed, their good work, and the bounce you get from that is priceless. A pat on the back is worth more than a raise, and it's cheaper to boot. Getting a note of thanks is low cost too, with high payback. People never forget what you do for them. Little things are actually big things.

And don't lose touch! I have friends I met once, twenty years ago, and we're still friends. I can still call them up, and I could walk into their office. The door would open, and they would say, "[Timothy L.], it's so good to see you! What can I do for you?" And it's all because they know I'd do the same for them, and probably have.

CHAPTER EIGHT

FIND GUARDIAN ANGELS AND BENEFACTORS

Guardian Angels and Benefactors

Angels and benefactors are people who believe in you, who watch out for you and have your best interests at heart.

When you have friends higher up the org chart, you are wrapped in a cloak of invincibility. You are more resistant to the daily fray in your department. When you present your ideas, people listen more closely and are more likely to believe you have the potential to say something valuable. When there is a fight or a dispute involving you, you are more likely to come out on top, because your friends rise quickly to your defense, and your enemies may think twice before going after you.

Having a benefactor starts with your boss. When your boss has your back, you get the benefit of the doubt from people up and down the food chain. Having the full faith and credit of your boss is a great foundation for your reputation. But the real trump card is to have real friends two and three clicks, or more, *up* the org chart.

However, knowing someone *distantly* up the chain of command may not serve your needs. Calling them in to sort out some small matter on your level will be seen as a waste of their time. Having friends at the top, when you're near the bottom, is like having a nuclear bomb—sure, you have it, but you can't really use it. A really big gun should be brought in only in the most dire of circumstances. Otherwise the benefit of angels and benefactors comes from access to information, advice, and counsel.

Problems with Mentors

The word "mentor" was inspired by Mentor, the trusted friend of Odysseus who was placed in charge of Odysseus's son's upbringing during his long absence while he went off to fight the Trojan War. The son, Telemachos, was visited by Athena who often disguised herself to appear to him as Mentor, offering sage advice and strategies to survive the intrigues surrounding him. So advice from a mentor has the tradition of being divinely inspired.

There is no word "mentee," although you see this back-formation everywhere; the proper word is "protégé." Although a mentor can be assigned by a third party, which fits the origins of the word, the best mentors are not assigned. The best mentor-protégé relationships grow up spontaneously, by mutual agreement of the two involved.

A mentor can smooth a young person's passage into and upward within an organization. Mentors can help orient a new person to the culture, practices, and mores of an organization and explain the unwritten rules that exist outside the employee manual. They can run interference for the inexperienced young person, solving problems he may encounter with personalities, codified rules, or business practices of all sorts. *And most important, they can mention your name when new assignments come up.*

A young person with *several* mentors in an organization is practically bulletproof. Not only can they bail you out of trouble, if you use them correctly, but they'll keep you from getting into trouble in the first place by offering good advice. If you have several lifelines to call when you don't know the right answer, a wise and knowledgeable advisor can help you get it right the first time.

Why would a mentor *volunteer* to assist a younger person when they don't have to do so? The reason is simple: *The mentor likes the protégé!* So it's important to be likeable. Protégés should also try to do favors for their mentors, because being useful creates a bond. In other cultures, protégés give gifts to their mentors, but in the United States or Canada, gifts of any significant value can appear to be bribes and so are not appropriate.

A word of caution as you develop mentor relationships: try to avoid using the word "mentor" at all. Call your friend a friend, an advisor, a connection you have higher up the food chain, an angel or benefactor, a person you can call on when you have certain types of questions about company practices, anything but the word "mentor." Some mentors are tired of the whole concept, because many organizations have overused the mentor-protégé relationship to try to improve onboarding and transfer of organizational culture. People who are regularly tapped to be mentors may be fatigued by *assigned* mentor-protégé relationships, and they may recoil at the thought of yet another protégé, especially if the last turned out to be a disappointment. Or they may still resent the prior ambitious clod who called constantly with trivial queries.

The following are the hallmarks of a good, *structured* mentoring program:

☐ Mentors are assigned by the organization; every incoming employee gets an assignment. No one is left out.

☐ Mentors are outside of the protégé's reporting chain, allowing more honest advice and counsel and reducing micromeddling. For example, mentors should be in the same division but in a different department from protégés, or in the same function but in different locations.

☐ Time for mentors and protégés to interact is structured into their schedules. There is an explicit minimum level of interaction.

☐ Mentors are either volunteers, who view mentoring and teaching as intrinsically rewarding activities, or directly compensated for mentoring, or both.

☐ There is a formal process in place for a protégé to switch from one mentor to another, without recriminations for either.

☐ Mentoring is factored into the review and advancement processes. If it is valued by the organization, mentors are rewarded for it.

Is It Best to Be Loved or Feared?

My father had a favorite saying: "If you want to sit at home and watch television, nobody is going to complain about you. But if you're going to do something in this world, someone's not going to like it." Highly successful people always generate some resentment, some friction within an organization. How is it best to diffuse or channel that resentment—by being charming and winning people into your favor or by channeling that resentment into the power you have over them?

In his famous treatise, *Il Principe*, the sixteenth-century Italian political theorist Niccolo Machiavelli analyzed the politics of power and decided that it is better to be feared than to be loved (for a prince, at least). He believed that leaders who are loved might get cooperation while times were good, but they could not count on compliance when times got rough. So being feared was a better control mechanism and thus a better choice for a leader who needed control. But does this type of control really matter in today's organizations? Should *you* be feared or loved?

When an org chart is flat, as most are today, any one person's power over another is diluted. This even applies to direct reports. If you have twenty direct reports, you're going to be much less involved in their daily lives than if you have three. And you need your workers. If you fire someone, you have to replace her, which can be expensive, time consuming, and risky.

By the way, you do have to fire someone occasionally as a leader and not just to get rid of bad people. Firing someone once in a while is an excellent way to keep subordinates interested in their jobs. But if you fire a lot of people, or fire people who are basically fulfilling their mission, you will have to spend a lot of your time on staffing rather than on the real work of your business unit.

People who are truly fulfilling their missions are not going to be afraid of being fired by you because they know you can't fire them because you can't afford to. So your biggest mechanism for creating fear is weakened. And today, employees have more power over their bosses than ever before. Once you reach a certain level, you can't get promoted without a 360° review. If your people hate you, they will be sure to nix your advancement, even if that means they have to continue to put up with you. Only landlords give good references for bad people.

When people fear you, they only do their work in response to that fear. Your method of control actually creates a need for that control. If they won't do anything without your direction, you're going to need to provide *a lot* of direction.

Douglas McGregor, an early business psychologist, codified this in his famous X and Y theory of management, presented in his landmark 1960 management book, *The Human Side of Enterprise.* X theory managers believe that people will not work without direct supervision and that people don't like to work anyway. Therefore an authoritarian management style, a militaristic command-and-control approach is the best way to get them to do work. Y theory managers believe that people work for their own internal reasons and that a manager's job is to foster and nurture that internal motivation and guide it to the enterprise's benefit. Thus a participative management style, one that allows information flows and power to go in all directions, is the best way to get them to do work.

Managers who believe in Y theory are more successful in knowledge organizations and in the flat org charts we all live with today. It is probably not very effective to *order* people to be creative or to *demand* that workers contribute good ideas. Y theory, with its collaborative and participatory management style, is not about being feared. Thus it would seem that it is best to be loved. But is it? When you are truly beloved, no one wants to see you go. They want to keep you close to them because they love you. You are the light of the department. If you were to leave, it would be the opposite of a cause for celebration; it would be a tragedy.

So being loved has a downside. If you're deeply integrated into your business unit, if you're embedded in it, if you're part of the source code, then you cannot be extracted without a high cost. Everybody has gone to going-away parties that were more like a wake than a celebration. If you're going to be deeply and truly missed, you may have waited too long to get promoted. You are perhaps too identified with the business unit you are leaving.

Because it is neither good to be feared nor beloved, the best management style is to be *well liked.*

Well-liked people get mentioned for promotion without excessive emotionality. Well-liked people are appreciated but not clung to, and being liked has the association of being well known and well respected.

It's a good idea to cultivate a little bit of a "just visiting" image. Let it be known that you are here to make some major contributions, but you should keep your boss on notice that you are not a lifer. You are going to do a great job while you're here, and you are going to be ready to hand that job off gracefully. The person who comes in behind you will be well set up to perform, because you know you will be leaving and you have put into place measures for a smooth transition.

Observations of a P.R. Account Executive

Recently I went to dinner in Baltimore with the account team for a sports drink. They had hired me to give a speech on career success to a trade group, and we were going to celebrate the fact that the talk had been well received. There were about fifteen of us at dinner, including a young woman who stood out noticeably from the rest. Her own boss deferred to her. Her own boss said she was lucky to have her services, while she could still afford her. The young woman was charming and funny, warm, the opposite of arrogant. She was obviously going places and maybe had one foot out the door already. And she was the epitome of well liked. Her compatriots knew that she was not going to be around long, and they liked her anyway, because she was hypercompetent, she did her job well, and she made their jobs easier at the same time. She had deflected any resentment that she might have engendered by being both socially adept and valuable to everyone on her team. That's the hallmark of a fast-track performer.

Having Business Friends: Make Them Before You Need Them

Guardian angels and benefactors aren't the only sources of power and effectiveness to be cultivated. Business friends, in general, can help you. Business friends may be found in other departments, other branches, and even other companies or industries. In short, they can be above, below, beside, or nearby you, and they needn't have positional power, either. Everybody knows the secretary or techie who can work magic; they have no positional authority, but they have huge value in helping you get your work done.

Having a wide network of business friends can help you find information and solve problems. Your friend in engineering can tell you whether a feature is feasible—while you're still in the client's office. Your friend in finance can tell if your division is slated for increased investment and happy times—or RIFS and divestiture. Your friend in another company can warn you about financial problems that threaten a customer's creditworthiness—alerting you to the need to change your terms with that account.

One huge rule about business friends, however, is this: **You have to make friends *before* you need them.** When you make friends only because of what they can do for you, you become known as a user. You have to *be* a friend to *have* a friend. You have to be useful, entertaining, charming, and supportive to have friends who are useful, entertaining, charming, and supportive.

This is akin to the rule of all politics: Doing favors for people is like money in the bank. You can call it in when you need it, but you have to do the favors *first*.

INTERVIEW WITH A CHIEF ENGINEER

Engineering is different from general management. For example, I make more decisions about whom to promote than almost any other kind of manager. We assemble project teams, and they each need a team leader, so in effect, that's elevating one person out of many, promoting them to be in charge. Engineers have to get used to competing for slots, and engineering managers have to get used to selecting people to be in charge.

The first thing I look for is technical knowledge. Engineers have a hard time working for someone who doesn't know as much as they do. If you pick someone who is really good from a business stand-point, you also have to be sure about the fundamentals.

For example, if the guys on the team ask the lead about tech specs, and the leader can't share useful information, then there's a problem. They do a lot of this in groups—they share knowledge and information—and when the leader can't deliver, if they don't know as much as the team working under them, that's bad. Techies have a hard time working for anyone who doesn't know the technology or the product.

Next I look for client skill. Everyone has clients, even if they are internal. So, you've got to have a leader who can interact with the customer. We lost a major contract before I came here, millions and millions of dollars to design a new control system for an aircraft, because some idiot built a team without a communicator. We ended up subbing for someone else on the same project, because we really did have the technology they needed, but we didn't win the contract.

I try not to promote someone who lacks basic engineering skill, and I try not to promote someone who can't tell me how they're going to solve the client problem. If you stink as a client guy, that's ok, but you better be ready to tell me how you're going to make that work out.

Either tell me who you're going to bring with you to handle the problem, or tell me how you're going to improve. I love engineers who go to Toastmasters. That tells me a lot about a guy.

Here's how I pick engineers to be promoted: I call them into a room, one by one, and ask them to assess the skills and strengths of their colleagues. What does this tell me? If people hate you, it's going to come out. And if people hate you, you can't lead them. Second, I get a clear idea of everyone's level of expertise. In effect, I get the team to pick its own leader, but I have a heavy hand in the process. I tell them my decision, but it came from them.

Sometimes promotions don't work out. There's no guarantee. And you have to be on top of things when that happens. You have to pull that guy out, or woman, whatever the case may be. That's always a disruption, but you have to do it and do it fast. Put them somewhere else, without destroying them. You can't lose good people, even if you make a mistake about an assignment. So even if you give someone a promotion, you have to be able to take it back, too. The best way to do that is blame a reorg, or tell them you are restructuring the work flow. Give them a chance to save face. Don't belittle them. You never know. Next year they might be able to handle a leadership role.

Here's my advice to young engineers trying to get ahead. It's a lot like getting an engineering job in the first place. You want to put it out there that you're going to give them the best return for their money, of anybody on the team that might be picked. You'd be surprised how many people don't consider that their boss is the one who's got the jobs and got the money, the one paying the bills, and they need to approach that boss like a company approaches a customer. ROI. Why you're the one who will maximize the outcome.

Oh, and there are the little things that add up to a reputation. Showing that you're looking out for the company, you believe in the company. You'd be surprised how many guys are always bad-mouthing the company. If you're with a company that you need to criticize, you need to get the hell out and go somewhere else. You want to show that you like the company, that you want to make it a better company, that you work for a company you can brag about. If you go to work every day with that kind of attitude, it shows.

And if you're one of these guys who wants to get promoted, people up the line need to know who you are. You need to get noticed. Just after I started here, I heard the president of the company was going to be in our facility. I made it a point to go up to him and shake his hand, and I wasn't going to miss a chance to do that. Later on he sent a nasty memo to my group, telling us how we had screwed up. I wrote him right back, reminding him that we had met and telling him how he was just flat-out wrong. And he was. I figured I wouldn't have a job by sundown the next day, but that was just the beginning of a relationship that has been gold for me.

He saved my butt several times. I survived several waves of layoffs. When we got new managers who came in and wanted to clean house and put in their own people, he'd send down an email, "No, you're not going to get rid of him." I've outlasted them all, and now I'm in charge. Know people up the ladder, and make sure they know you, too.

CHAPTER NINE

MOVE—DAMMIT—AND HERE'S WHY

Do You Have a Career or a Lifestyle?

Do you have a career or do you have a lifestyle? Having a career means having a series of jobs chosen very intentionally to develop your skills and increase your rank and responsibilities. Having a lifestyle is to spend that same planning energy on your toys and privileges and station in life. The real point is: What is your goal? What is your real motivation? Career advancement? Or lifestyle advancement?

Having a career is not just about having an important position. Some very successful people don't have a career. They took a disjointed series of positions out of whim, luck, or necessity, and through some level of innate intelligence, talent, and drive, succeeded in each assignment. But they had no intentional progression.

Incidentally, some people with very modest positions are very much careerists. A truck driver studying for a Haz Mat credential and planning on qualifying to drive doubles is managing his career, while a VP of marketing who spends all of her time thinking about decorating her summer home and shaving a few strokes off her golf score has a lifestyle.

What is your goal, and what is your motivation? If your goal is your career, you should realize that moving around the country, and even taking offshore assignments, are required for rapid, uninterrupted career advancement. A slavish devotion to location is almost always a sign that you value your lifestyle more than you value your career.

One of the ways that fast-track careerists differ from regular people is that they wring every chance for advancement out of an employer before they separate from that employer and move on. If you won't relocate, you can't extract every opportunity from an employer that they have to offer.

There's nothing wrong with choosing lifestyle over career, but be sure you realize it is a choice. Make that choice with intention rather than bumbling into a decision with ramifications that you have not fully sorted out.

The Two-Turndown Rule

Most companies have a "two-turndown rule." If you turn down one promotion, the next reassignment offer you receive will be your last. If you turn that one down, you will retire in place, if you don't get fired. Some companies, especially vibrant, rapid-growth companies, have a *one* turndown rule. Turn them down once, and you are off the fast track and may be derailed altogether.

These are not written, codified H.R. rules but simply long established corporate practices. It's one of those cases where no one could point to the rule that says this, but everyone knows the rule.

Interview with Safety Engineer, Justin H.

"I got hired in Little Rock, and pretty quickly took a promotion that involved moving my family to Ohio. I thought it was okay, but my wife was unhappy. She wanted some part-time work and never found any. We'd never lived through a winter like that, and the kids got teased in school for being different. So I put in for a transfer back. It was a lateral, but I took it. Now I can tell my status has changed in the company. They don't ask my advice. I don't get assigned to task forces. It's like I'm invisible. I'll definitely have to change employers to advance."

See the Bigger Picture

Before you think about turning down a promotion offer, remember the two- (or one-) turndown rule. See the bigger picture of your future with this employer, and don't decide based on the immediate assignment but based upon the impact to your career with that employer.

Being open to living somewhere new can also help you start on a faster track according to Alan D. Ferrell, placement director at the Krannert School of Management at Purdue University. "Some students are interested in staying near home and family or living in a particular urban area. But even if you start out where you want, you may end up moving and being disappointed later in your career," he says. "Being prepared to relocate often, especially early in your career, builds a tremendous advantage five years out."

The U.S. Bureau of Labor Statistics tracks tenure with employers. For workers early in their careers, it is less than four years. When workers switch employers, they often trade locales at the same time.

If you are going to relocate sooner or later anyway, you may as well relocate when it first comes up, when it has a chance to enhance your career rather than hinder it. *Early career success compounds the most.* Move early, and you can have a higher chance of living wherever you want, later on. Moving later just because you're desperate to revive an endangered career is better than dying in place but not nearly as smart as getting an early jumpstart on others.

Give Your Employer a Chance to Make You Delighted

When you first hear of a potential relocation, you may have an instant reaction, "Oh, no. Not *there!*" But give your employer a chance to make the deal work for you. First of all, be sure you understand the career opportunity.

Scenario #1

Boss: "Would you like to go to Dusty Nowhere, about thirty miles from the border and at least two hundred miles from a business-class hotel? You'll be working with rattlesnakes."

You: "No way!"

Boss: "Okay, we'll ask Mandy over here if she wants to do it."

Scenario #2

Boss: "Would you like to go to Dusty Nowhere, about thirty miles from the border and at least two hundred miles from a business-class hotel? You'll be working with rattlesnakes."

You: "Maybe. Tell me what's involved. I'd like to know more."

Boss: "You will be host of a television pilot on parties and festivals of the world. The first one you'll cover is the Rattlesnake Roundup near Dusty Nowhere. After that we're going to send you to Oktoberfest in Munich and Carnival in Rio. Your compensation will be ten times as much as you make now, and if the pilot gets picked up, you'll be rich *and* famous. There's potential for spin-offs and licensing, and you'll get a percentage all down the line. The CEO is throwing his whole weight behind this project."

Obviously, you need to know what the opportunity is in terms of the assignment. And you also need to know what the opportunity is in terms of its long-term career value to you. How will this assignment develop you and position you for continued success? That's how you make your decision. Smart careerists always look five years ahead, one or two steps past the job in front of them.

When you take a relocation assignment, there will be opportunities to renegotiate almost every aspect of your employment relationship, starting with your title and compensation. There also will be opportunities for education benefits, such as private school tuition for your children, or trailing spouse services to help your partner in life find professional employment in the new locale. You might bring an elderly parent with you and need to set up care arrangements. You can negotiate relocation allowances, time in a corporate apartment to get your bearings in the new community, assistance in purchasing a new home, and help selling your old home. You can negotiate benchmark bonuses, as in "I'd like to get a $10,000 performance bonus the day the store opens, if it opens on schedule." Even an entry-level person can negotiate for ninety days in a corporate apartment, plus all relocation expenses.

You can also negotiate the duration of the assignment and try to extract explicit promises of rewards for taking the assignment. "I'll go open these ten stores for you, but I want a guarantee that I'll get named regional merchandiser at the end of the project."

One warning about promises: A boss or an H.R. officer trying to fill an assignment may be rather cavalier with promises, especially if the assignment is critical or difficult to fill. You may be promised things that later fail to materialize. At the very least, get all promises in writing. Ask for a memo that can go, officially, into your personnel file. You should say: "I would like you to put that in a memo that I can have put in my personnel file. Is that okay with you?"

If the promises are broken, *do not make a big deal out of it*. Business realities change, and promises made under one set of circumstances may not be appropriate or possible to honor under different circumstances. Being rigid is a career stopper, and being flexible is a career asset. Being flexible allows you to search for more than one path to success.

No matter what any employer does to you, I like to apply the stock holding rule: Would you buy this stock today at this price? If the answer is yes, you keep it. If the answer is no, then you sell it and reinvest elsewhere. The same rule applies in careers. Would you take this job today? Is it a good opportunity, looking forward? If the answer is yes, you forgive your employer all past transgressions and move forward. If that answer is no, you start to look around for a better investment.

Relocation Calculators

When negotiating the terms of a relocation assignment, be sure to be mindful of the different costs of living around the country. Two cities thirty miles apart may have vastly different cost profiles. Is a salary of $50,000 a year in Dallas more than $100,000 in San Francisco? Maybe. The way to find out is to use one of the many good regionalized salary, cost of living, and relocation calculators available on the Internet. Here are a few to evaluate:

http://jobstar.org/tools/salary/index.php
www.salary.com
www.payscale.com
www.salaryexpert.com

www.homefair.com
www.stevensworldwide.com
www.bekinsmoving.com
www.bankrate.com
www.quintcareers.com/relocation_resources.html

There are dozens more reputable sites, and certainly you should use more than one.

The tax structure and the cost of housing are only parts of the equation. For example, in one city you may have to put your children in private school, whereas another has a perfectly satisfactory public school system. That's a *huge* cost differential that won't show up in most relocation analyses. Design your own cost comparisons based on how you actually live.

How I Got to San Francisco in the First Place

My first job out of college was as a resume writer in Seattle. Although my father was an entrepreneur and I had grown up around business all my life, I had rebelled by majoring in philosophy and religion. I didn't know much about resumes, I assure you. Later I got a master's degree in human resources and organization development, but at the time I really had to talk my way into this first job. The hiring officer was another resume writer, but he wanted to work on his novel more than he wanted to do his work. I told him if he hired me today, he could go back to his novel writing without worrying another minute about this placement. So he hired me on the spot.

I immediately got my own office in the Smith Tower, suite 2001, one of the oldest skyscrapers west of the Mississippi. With no training whatsoever, my assignment was to help people take a rough draft of a resume and make it into a passable business document. I knew only a little about business but a lot about writing, so I bought every career book on the market and read all of them. Almost all my business was by referral. I'd help one person, and she'd send me four of her friends. I was doing so well that the regional manager came up to meet me.

"You're the best guy we've ever had in this office," he told me. "Well," I said, "Maybe I need a better office. What's the best office in the United States?" He said it was in the Financial District in San Francisco. I begged for the assignment. "No way!" he said. "You're too new, and besides, the guy in that office has been there for six years, and he's not going anywhere." I told him I would jump at the chance to have the best office in the country.

Literally, one week later, he called me on a Tuesday morning. "The guy quit, and he gave only a week's notice! I'm really in a bind. Let's see if you're serious. If you can be in San Francisco on Monday morning at 9 o'clock, you can have the assignment." *While we were talking on the phone, I accepted, changing my life forever.* I relocated with five days notice.

I worked in Seattle until Friday at five and drove to San Francisco, moved into a hotel, and met him at my new office at 9 a.m. Monday. It was the best move of my life and critical for everything that I have been able to accomplish since then.

A Warning about Children

Sociologists tell us that children acclimate to peers and the social practices and mores of their surroundings. Rather than adopt their parents' values and worldview wholesale, they *mostly* adapt to the larger society they grow up in, the one outside their homes. This is obviously a survival mechanism. Parents will pass on eventually, and children need to survive and succeed in the social world that they find themselves in rather than the social world that their parents brought with them.

In any single generation, any family can become locals, anywhere. Think about George Bush the Elder, very much a reserved, patrician, old-money Yankee New Englander, and his son, George Bush the Younger, a cowboy-boot-wearing, aw-shucks Texan through and through. Both were authentic representations of their origins in just one generation.

Think about this before you raise children in Lower Windswept Nowhere or Inner Urban Hell. One top executive I interviewed for this book took an assignment as plant manager of a chemical processing plant along the Mississippi River, more than a hundred miles from a department store. He was distraught that his daughter was dating the high school football quarterback. "She's happy because he's the quarterback, and all I can see is a future roustabout," he lamented to me over a late night Scotch. Another executive I interviewed sent his daughter to boarding school after a teen pool party in a foreign country where he was assigned at the time. "I looked around that crowd and saw all those potential boyfriends and sent her off to boarding school in the United States."

A year or two in any locale will be an enriching experience, but middle school through high school, and that is going to be where your children are from forever.

Who's Provincial?

The word "provincial" comes from the word "provinces," as in people from the provinces. Supposedly, people from the provinces are naïve, unschooled, and unaware of the greater world outside their village. I find the most provincial people in this country, however, to be lifelong urbanites, especially those who are still living in the same urban area where they grew up and inhabiting the exact same class and social position as their parents. Some of them are naïve, unschooled, and unaware of the greater world outside of their village!

If you are afraid to live among the people in the flyover states, you are missing a chance to learn about your fellow citizens and the people who will buy your products and services. If you don't understand your markets, you are not going to make it to the top.

Two-Career Families

Many young people today can expect to be part of a two-career family unit, which brings some challenges to the relocation equation. The real problems arise when both parties have careers of about equal potential. Sometimes one partner deserves the nod, sometimes the other. Certainly a woman who compromises every time will find herself at a distinct income disadvantage in the future, particularly if there is a divorce. I know this sounds pessimistic, but statistically, half of all marriages in the United States end in divorce, so it is something to take into consideration when making career moves.

On this two-income family issue I do want to make one point very strongly: Men cannot expect women to compromise on their careers over and over and then fail to compensate them for that if they do get divorced. You cannot ask for a 1950s marriage and then demand a new millennium divorce. (Of course, high-earning women cannot do this, either.)

If one of the parties is a fast-track executive, or even just earns many times more than the other, it makes sense to make that person's career the one around which to build compromises. This can be a gender issue but doesn't have to be. It doesn't matter who is the top earner.

It helps if one of the partners has a job that can be found in any locale, such as accounting or teaching school. A relocation is not going to derail these types of careers, which can be relocated and resumed elsewhere with minimal penalty. In fact, occasional relocation may result in *increased* success for a trailing spouse, if he or she is packaged correctly. Trailing spouse services are a common part of any executive relocation. Trailing spouse services may involve career counseling, resume preparation, and even personal introduction to appropriate local employers.

In general, the keys to keeping a two-career family going are compromise and communication. Sit down with this chapter and talk about it. A little horse trading and quid pro quo may not be a bad approach.

Living Apart, Managing Remotely, and Big-Time Commuting

I never saw an oft removed tree,
Nor yet an oft removed family,
That throve so well as those that settled be.
And again, three removes is as bad as a fire,
And again, keep the shop, and thy shop will keep thee.

—BENJAMIN FRANKLIN

There you have it. Three moves is about the same as a house fire. Ripping up home and hearth every year or two is particularly expensive and has ramifications for wealth accumulation. Real estate transactions, redecorating, uncompensated moving expenses, damage to heirloom furniture, episodic spousal unemployment, and so on, all add up. And relocating from high-cost areas to low-cost areas, and vice versa, involves some particularly delicate calculations of risk and benefit.

One solution to relocation strains for two-career families, especially those with children at critical educational junctures, is to commute. Commuting is particularly appropriate when the assignment may take less than two years, or if the assignment is so risky it may fail altogether.

With the technology in place to allow telecommuting, noncolocated teams, and virtual management, even the most ambitious executives can be effective remotely at least part of the time. This changes the equation of commuting and allows any worker to work in one part of the country and live in another. Careerists have been successful with workstyles that were unheard of before the last few years: in the office three weeks a month and home one week a month; in the office Monday through Thursday, and home every weekend; remix ad infinitum.

One client of mine was president of a company in San Jose, California, while his family lived in a suburb of Chicago. With children in high school, his wife refused to move "one more time." He was home most weekends, his kids were doing well, and his wife was much happier than she would have been had she had to move.

Another client of mine had an elegant, executive home in the Silicon Valley. He was offered an assignment as CFO in a lower-cost area of Florida. He was afraid if he sold out of the California real estate market it would cost him a fortune to buy back in later, and his wife owned a business that could not be relocated. He commuted for two years rather than risk selling his home and selling off his wife's business. The company paid for his Florida apartment and all his airline tickets. When the Florida business unit was sold, he returned to HQ with nary a financial or logistical problem.

Why You Can't Afford to Be Provincial

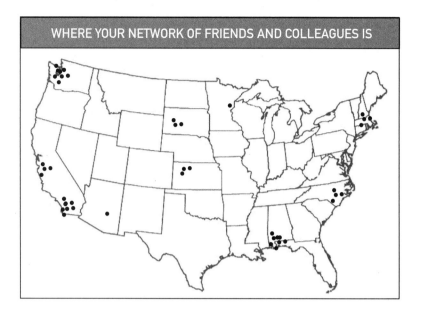

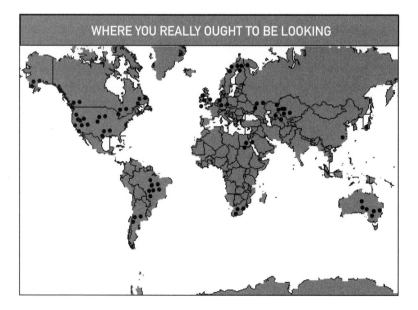

One of my best friends has a very successful career with an organization that uses a core-hours model. At his company, all meetings are scheduled on Tuesday, Wednesday, or Thursday between 10 and 3. He has a beautiful home in a serene and tranquil area outside of town and closer to his wife's work, and he keeps an apartment in the city. He works from home unless a meeting is called that involves him.

(These types of commuting arrangements are appropriate for highly valued employees well into their careers. In most cases, young people who have not yet differentiated themselves are better off going down to the office and showing face.)

One careerist I interviewed for this book had a very unusual work- and lifestyle: He and his wife had *never* lived in the same city. He was forty when he married for the first time, to a woman who also had never been married before. She was a scientist in Reno, Nevada, and he was a faculty member with tenure at a Florida university. With the frequent breaks in the academic calendar, they were together about as much as any marriage of two Type A careerists. "It keeps a marriage fresh," he confided.

Offshore Assignments

Offshore assignments are now a critical part of executive development. In the global market reality of our day, if you are headed for the top you need to prove yourself successful in an offshore setting. The trend is toward more travel and extended but temporary visits, and less outright relocation to another country. Either way, you need this rotation on your resume.

Ex-pat compensation packages are complex and hefty. If you have a residential assignment involving a family relocation, it may involve housing; club memberships; local "American school" expenses for your children; replacement of lost spousal income; additional vacation to match local norms; a cadre of coaches, consultants, and language tutors; and on-demand, first-class air tickets for you and all your family to ease adjustment, deal with family emergencies, or just because.

"Grossing up" refers to the process of raising your package of compensation and benefits to match the *higher* of two norms—the *disposable* income you would expect to earn for such a position in the United States or the *disposable* income someone would expect to earn for such a position in the destination country. Taxation and compensation practices vary widely worldwide, and analysis needs to take into account practices that are not easily comparable. For example, salaries in Japan are modest, but Japanese benefits would make the most avaricious American blush, including extravagantly expensive club memberships and even late-night "entertainment" for one's associates. And the first $82,400 in offshore income is federal tax free, even if the check is signed in New York.

Some places to research this further include:

www.expatica.com
www.expatfocus.com
http://www.expatfinancial.com/links.htm

There are H.R. consulting firms that specialize in coaching U.S. citizens (and their families) to prepare for successful offshore assignments. Their services include everything from pre-assignment planning, through schools selection, to which activities a spouse might want to get involved in, to repatriation. *It is highly recommended that you seek and acquire such assistance.*

Start with a test of your compatibility and suitability for an offshore assignment. These tests exist for the executive herself and for all the members of her family. United States citizens have an infamously high failure rate offshore. They fail in three distinct ways: They fail to be successful with their foreign counterparts, due to cultural insensitivity and a lack of language skills. They fail to thrive, and quit or demand a return. Or their family does not adjust, leading to children acting out, resentful spouses, and even divorce.

One final warning about an offshore assignment: Once you are overseas, you disappear from the daily flow of gossip, tips, and information floating around any organization. You run the risk of suffering from the truth of the old maxim "Out of sight, out of mind." When you return, your hard work and great contributions may not be known to or valued by the domestic officers to whose world you are returning. And worst of all, there may be no good slot for you to return to!

To combat this, you must stay in close contact with people at HQ. Lose sleep if necessary to have frequent conference calls, or better yet, videoconferences where you can see and be seen. Come home several times a year to make reports in person, and stay extra days to find out what's going on in the business units that you care about. Finally, ask for what you want! At least six months before you intend to return, start lobbying for an appropriate position.

Otherwise, your important and necessary career development may turn out to be for the benefit of another company—a company that you join after you get frustrated at your lack of reward and decide to leave.

INTERVIEW WITH A CFO, CLAYTON M.

The hardest jump I made was the first one, from being a team member to being a supervisor. I almost failed at it, really. In college I [had been in a fraternity], a group of really close guys, and when I went to work I naturally took that mentality with me. I believed in camaraderie. I believed in watching your brother's back. I enjoyed the fun of being young in New York, too. New York really is the greatest city in the world, and there's no better place that I know of for it to be 5 o'clock. People in my office didn't work late. On my floor we had a rule. You couldn't leave before the senior person on the floor. But the minute the doors of the elevator closed behind him, the department emptied out.

I wanted to advance, and I talked my way into a promotion to supervisor. My work was good, without question, but I didn't know anything about leadership. I didn't understand anything at all about setting standards, about giving direction, or about solving problems that people have with each other. I made the mistake of thinking that because these people were my friends, they'd do the right thing.

Most of all, I wanted things to stay the same. I went to the same bars with the same group of people. I tried to stay in the 5 o'clock club. I actually believed it would *help* me manage well if I was friends with the people on my team. Well, that turned out to be a mistake.

My "friends" pulled every stupid and juvenile stunt on me you can imagine. Little by little I was losing control over my team. Luckily my manager diagnosed my problem. He called me aside and said what I was doing was not going to work out. He said leading by example was a myth, that in the military they had explained to him that leading by example gets the lead man killed. It's not leadership at all. You have to provide direction and demand accountability. He signed me up for supervisory training, and he gave me another chance.

Pretty quickly I learned to pay more attention to my bosses than to my peers. I started to identify with senior management and not the worker bees. I finally saw who my real constituency was. The people I needed to impress were not the people working for me but the people I worked *for*. You can't be everyone's friend. This is all obvious to me now, but it wasn't then.

I have two other points for your readers. One is that you will keep developing over your career, or more accurately, you *have to* keep developing over your career. I have skills now I didn't even understand existed three or four assignments back. And I'm not talking about technical skills. There actually is such a thing as refining your judgment, getting seasoned in a role. There is such a thing as wisdom.

I think for the jump into the executive team, the biggest difference was how public things become. You can't hide things so much. You'd better not fake things. You shouldn't be doing those things anyway. I have no idea how they pulled off WorldCom for so long. Enron I get. That was off balance sheet. But either way, you couldn't do these types of things where I've worked. Transparency is an ideal, and what passes for standard operating procedure is certainly less than that, but let me say this, you have to be more careful. You might hire an accounting manager based on a referral and good resume, but a

CFO, or any top officer, has got to be ready to be checked out thoroughly. That's not to say they always do it, check them out, I mean, but just because it might happen, it changes the equation. Things you might have tried to hide or gloss over at a lower level are likely to be exposed. You get more and more honest, especially as you move upward. I'm not talking about middle management, but that's the price of admission to the top floor. Greater accountability. I made a few mistakes. My rule now is simple: Never hide critical information from those above you. It's not a bad thing, necessarily. But you do have to know about it, see it coming, and keep your ducks in a row.

CHAPTER TEN

FIND THE RIGHT MIX OF PREPARED AND LUCKY

What about Luck?

Top executives attribute a higher percentage of their success to luck than do middle managers. I think they must be accurate in their assessments. Talent and drive and hard work are like seeds on the ground; no matter how good those seeds are they need a little rain from above. They need a break from forces they can't control.

Luck is an odd force in the world. Luck is not random. Luck can be prepared for. It can be pushed a little. If the soil in one place is not right, move your seeds. If it doesn't rain this year, eat from your stores and prepare for next year. Almost all agrarian societies have some kind of rain dance, or rain ceremony, because they believe luck can be lobbied. *The best way to lobby luck is to be ready for its arrival.*

For example, it tends to rain at the same time each year, more or less. If you anticipate luck, like a farmer anticipates rain, and have your seeds in the ground on time, you will be ready for it to rain. Luck rewards those who prepare. It is not random in its effect. As a careerist I once interviewed told me: "The more prepared I get, the luckier I am." You need the right mix of prepared and lucky, methodical and nimble, and luck will be kind to you.

In my own assessment of career progression, luck, also known as chance, plays a huge part in actual careers. We are all, perhaps, too enamored of the whole concept of career planning: I'll do this, then I'll get that training, and I'll qualify to do that, leading to an opportunity as. . . . We especially drill this into our college seniors and young MBAs. Plan your work, and work your plan. Know where you're going. Don't just jump off the diving board without thoroughly researching the water in the pool. Be careful! Fear risk! Assess your odds!

But you can plan only so much—sometimes things just happen. In fact, people who methodically follow their plans, no matter what, won't get very far. You don't become a corporate officer before age forty by being safe, conservative, methodical, and plodding. Whenever you see a thirty-four-year-old officer, you know she didn't get there by sticking to her original plan!

As they say in the Marines, sometimes you have to improvise.

So how do you factor luck into career planning?

We have spent most of this book working up the case *for* career planning. You need to take care of your skillset. You need to constantly learn and evolve. You need to see, admit, and compensate for your weaknesses. Let us now focus on the rest of the equation: being lucky and nimble.

Chutzpah from a Banker: James G.

"When I was twenty-three years old, the director of the marketing department at a small regional bank had just departed, and his function was in disarray. I had been with the bank less than a year. I just walked in to the president's office and said, "I want this. I can do this." He said, "Be careful what you ask for!" So at the ripe old age of twenty-three, I was put in charge of a staff of twenty-five and a million-dollar budget. Maybe he thought I'd fail, but instead my career took off like a rocket. I had friends with fancier jobs, but within a couple years I was way ahead of them. You gotta ask to get, that's what I say. That's what my father taught me.

"Why do people get passed over? The opposite of chutzpah, I suppose, is timidity. And that's not a personality characteristic that sells.

If every time you face three choices, you take the least risky and most defensible, well that gets noticed if it's a pattern.

"Also—and this is a biggie—I call it the hygiene factor. There's the obvious part of this, the spinach salad rule: never eat a spinach salad for an interview because you'll have green teeth. But it is bigger than clothes and manners and going out to dinner and that type of thing. It also includes whether you are inarticulate, if your written work is an embarrassment, if your physical presentation is not crisp, if in your professional life there's a lack of discipline and work. Nobody wants to associate with someone whose work *and work habits* do not reflect the image they want to have associated with their company.

"So, in short, being too conservative and risk averse, and being sloppy, are why people get passed over.

"H.R. people are the last people who know who should be promoted and why. You go where the hurt is and talk to the people closest to the problem, people responsible for actual work. Forget about H.R. You've got to ask for what you want. No one's going to come looking for you."

Don't Be Afraid to Fail

Whether you like it or not there's no such thing as a low-risk career. Loyal plodders are laid off along with star performers, so you may as well go for it! Five years after he graduated from college, Bobby J. oversaw a $4 billion budget and 23,000 employees as secretary of the department of health and hospitals for the State of Louisiana. He definitely didn't get there by playing it safe. Here's what he has to say: "Don't be afraid to fail. Too often we aim for the middle because we don't want to deal with spectacular success or failure. But we can only stretch ourselves by aiming for things that we don't know if we can do. It's too easy to settle into a comfortable, stable job. But if you don't take risks when you're young and have the ability to adapt, you're not going to take them later, when you really need to.

How Far Ahead Can You Plan?

Careerists—those who have intentional careers rather than a series of jobs—plan deeper than regular people. They *position* themselves for success in the future. They develop their skillsets, meet the right people, and accumulate the right mix of diverse experiences to advance up the org chart. But how far ahead, really, can you plan?

Anyone who is not looking two positions ahead is not looking far enough. For a fast-track careerist, that's somewhere between two and five years. So that's the near horizon for a thoughtful person. But what's the far horizon?

It seems pretty clear to me that the career-planning horizon is no more than twenty years. After that, you're dealing with mostly fiction and fantasy. Think about it. The Internet is less than twenty years old. Bill Gates started the software industry and became the richest man in the world in less than twenty years. All the information you would use for planning is probably going to change anyway over any twenty-year span. We are poised on revolutions in biotech, nanotech, geopolitics, the environment, and religion that will change everything we know and believe within this coming twenty years.

Your job may become obsolete. Laws may change, destroying your market. Your industry may move offshore. Public tastes may change, eliminating a need for your services altogether. I used to have a boss who was fond of telling all his employees, "You can be replaced by a button." His point was that no one was indispensable, but in time maybe some of those old jobs will, literally, be replaced by a button.

Look as deep as you can, five to ten years at least, but know that around twenty years, all bets will be off.

Don't Slap Opportunity in the Face

Opportunity is all around us, all the time. You just have to learn to see it.

My father was a serial entrepreneur. He could make more money on a street corner than most people could with a whole store. During the Korean War, when he was on leave in Seoul, he noticed that every soldier who got off the plane had to have one of those little rectangular shoulder bags that used to be called airline bags. But instead of buying his bag from a vendor for $2, he bought his airline bag for a pack of cigarettes from a soldier headed *back* from leave. Airline bags were de rigueur for leave, but they had no value whatsoever on the front lines, where cigarettes were the currency.

My father spent most of his leave in the airport, buying airline bags for packs of cigarettes and selling them for $2 apiece. He threw in a few recommendations for free about where to go in Seoul.

After the war, he started several companies, none of which grew particularly big, but all of which were fun and sold for a profit. My father made money seemingly just by breathing. Even his hobbies and pastimes were profitable. He's retired now, but he still cannot resist exploiting market inefficiencies.

Opportunity is all around you, but you have to be able to recognize it. One thing about opportunity, though, is that it is like an easily offended paramour. If you don't *see* and *appreciate* her, it is like you slapped her in the face. She is gone.

You need to learn to develop contingency plans for your plans and to model multiple scenarios with more variables in play. You need to learn to pay attention to those with power and potential. If you unexpectedly gain access to people with great power or great potential, *quickly* develop a plan to capitalize on that contact. ***Learn to consider options that you had not anticipated.*** That's the biggest key of all.

Taking a Sudden Turn

Things happen. I had a client who chatted up her seatmate on an airplane and ended up with a job in a new industry. She had never thought about that industry for a second before that conversation, yet it resulted in an officer-level hire. You just can't plan for things like that.

Another client was looking for a new job because she was stuck in a dead-end division of a tech company. We had been practicing elevator speeches for her to use in networking. An elevator speech is a standard tool for jobseekers. It is what you would say to Bill Gates, or some other luminary, if he got on an elevator with you and you had about four to six floors to make your pitch. In as few words as possible, it's who you are, what you can do, and what kind of opportunity you are looking for.

So she gets on an elevator at work and looks at the badge of the guy that got on with her, *and he's a top company officer.* It was a cliché come true. She launches into her elevator speech, in an actual elevator, and he invites her to call him. She did and managed to extract one more promising assignment from this company.

ESPN analyst Doris Burke got her start in front of the cameras when an announcer didn't show up for a men's game. At the last minute, they grabbed her from a supporting role and placed her in front of the camera, and she was instantly a star. Did she plan that? Absolutely not.

Dick Cheney gave a graduation speech at LSU highlighting exactly this point: "On the day of my own graduation at the University of Wyoming, I had no ambition for public life. . . . Many of you will leave LSU today with definite plans of your own. Setting a plan for your life can be a good thing. It keeps you focused on the future and gives you a standard against which you can measure your progress. Yet I'll wager that ten years from now, many of you will find yourselves following a very different course, all because of an opportunity that came to you out of the blue. Be on watch for those certain moments, and certain people, that come along and point you in a new direction." That's sage advice for all of us.

A person I interviewed for this book converted a wrong number into a promotion! Someone called him by mistake because he had a similar name to someone much more important in the company. He was friendly with the caller, and joked about this happening all the time. He managed to get a conversation going, and bang, he gets an introduction to a senior person that within a month resulted in a promotion to a new assignment. There is no way to plan for that.

Unlikely introductions are a mainstay of networking lore. A friend of mine got a job as second unit director on a movie in L.A. because he had the same dog walker as the producer. You don't plan stuff like that—*you see it and capitalize on it.* So in spite of all the planning mentioned in this book, let chance play its part. ***See opportunity and capitalize on it,*** especially if it comes from an unexpected source!

Thank You

Thank you very much for reading this little tome. I hope it is useful to you, and helps you get promoted again and again. Send your business stories to don@donaldasher.com. I may not be able to reply, but I promise you, I read them all. Career blessings to you,

Don Asher

Donald M. Asher is one of America's premier career consultants, specializing in the hidden job market and the self-directed job search, and a nationally recognized speaker at colleges and conferences coast to coast.

He is also the author of nine other books, all published by Ten Speed Press:

Cool Colleges
How to Get Any Job with Any Major
Asher's Bible of Executive Résumés
The Overnight Résumé
From College to Career
Graduate Admissions Essays
The Overnight Job Change Strategy
The Overnight Job Change Letter
The Foolproof Job-Search Workbook

In addition, Donald Asher is a contributing writer for the *San Francisco Chronicle, San Francisco Examiner,* the *Wall Street Journal*'s CareerJournal.com and CollegeJournal. com, Monster's monstertrak.com, *The National Business Employment Weekly, Managing Your Career Magazine, NACE Journal, WACE Spotlight,* jobstar.org, wetfeet.com, MSN Encarta, and many other publications and career sites.

Also by Donald Asher

Cool Colleges

For the Hyper-Intelligent, Self-Directed, Late-Blooming, and Just Plain Different

COOL COLLEGES is an in-depth look at the best-kept secrets in higher education today

Fully revised and updated since the 2000 edition, COOL COLLEGES profiles more than 40 innovative and unorthodox schools and provides an insider's edge on how to apply to and get accepted at the school that's right for you.

COOL COLLEGES is the only resource that reveals the schools that:

- *don't* want your SAT scores
- are *so* competitive they reject more than 90% of applicants
- graduate the most millionaires
- don't give grades
- are *totally* free

The new edition also includes a brand new chapter dedicated to eco schools and the latest ranking information on the hottest schools in the country today. COOL COLLEGES is a must for the independently minded.

$21.95 paperback (Can $26.95)
ISBN-13: 978-1-58008-839-8

How to Get Any Job

Life Launch and Re-Launch for Everyone Under 30 (or How to Avoid Living in Your Parents' Basement)

$15.99 paperback (Can $19.99)
ISBN-13: 978-1-58008-947-0

Available from Ten Speed Press wherever books are sold.

TEN SPEED PRESS
Berkeley
www.crownpublishing.com
www.tenspeed.com